Modern Literature and the Religious Frontier

NATHAN A. SCOTT, JR.

Modern Literature and the Religious Frontier

HARPER & BROTHERS
NEW YORK

809.04

Scol m

Library of Congress catalog card number: 58–7476

38339

Oct. 1959

To REINHOLD NIEBUHR

From whom I learned my first
lessons in detecting the religious frontiers
of contemporary culture—

Whose classroom was for me
the place of the first Great Awakening

Contents

Contents

Preface

Unlike such men of our day as T. S. Eliot and Allen Tate and W. H. Auden, whose inquiries into the nature of man's life in culture have led them often to move from a consideration of aesthetic and literary problems to a consideration of religious and theological problems, I have myself been led in recent years, with increasing regularity, to move from theological problems to literary and aesthetic problems, and this little book is a kind of interim report on a journeying that is still in progress. It was in the mid-'forties that I first began to be propelled in this direction—as a result, I suspect, of insights that had been won both in theology and in modern literature. In the first instance, my theological studies had gradually deepened in me the conviction that a major task of Christian theology in our time (as in all previous times) is to negotiate a continuous conversation between the faith of which it is a custodian and the world of contemporary culture in which this faith must have its actual life. And I came to this position not simply for tactical reasons dictated by the exigencies of the apologetic situation, but rather because this was a view of the relation of faith to culture that seemed to be required by the very nature of Christian theology itself. For to be in the situation of faith is to be in the situation at once of asking questions about the meaning of human existence and of imaginatively beholding the revelatory event (which, for Christian faith, is the divine self-manifestation that occurred in the appearance of Jesus as the Christ) wherein those questions are answered. And it is the task of theology to establish the relations between the questions that are proposed out of man's cultural existence and the answers to those questions that are given in the *kerygma* (the Christian message). Indeed, as Professor Paul Tillich has reminded us, "the term 'theo-logy' implies, as such, a mediation, namely, between the mystery, which is *theos,* and the understanding, which is *logos."* [1]* "The answers implied in the event of revelation are meaningful," he says,

> only in so far as they are in correlation with questions concerning the whole of our existence, with existential questions. Only those who have experienced the shock of transitoriness, the anxiety in which they are aware of their finitude, the threat of nonbeing, can understand what the notion of God means. Only those who have experienced the tragic ambiguities of our historical existence and have totally questioned the meaning of existence can understand what the symbol of the Kingdom of God means. Revelation answers questions which have been asked and always will be asked because they are "we ourselves." [2]

Now this means that constructive Christian thought must always be "anthropological," in the broadest sense, as well as radically "theological." It must *begin,* that is, with man and with all those dimensions of his experience in which he has discovered his existence to be fundamentally problematic: it originates in an analysis of the human situation on the basis of "materials made available by man's creative self-interpretation in all realms of culture." [3] The theological community must, in other words, enter into a dialogical relationship with philosophy, with the social sciences, with therapeutic psychology, with imaginative literature—and it must do this because of the very nature of Christian theology itself; for, though the content of the Christian faith can never be derived from an analysis of human existence (since it represents something " 'spoken to' human existence from beyond it" [4]), this "content" is itself never something absolutely discarnate, and its "form" is always determined by the nature of the questions upon which the kerygma must be brought to bear. It is, indeed, just at this point that we may see most clearly why it is that one major aspect of the theological task must always have to do with the whole set of problems constituting the field of what is perhaps best called the "theology of culture." And it was this recognition (toward which I was greatly assisted by Professor Tillich) that marked a decisive stage in the development of my own theological thought.

But, then, being of an incurably apologetic temper and never having had any real inclination, vocationally, toward the disciplines of kerygmatic theology, when I began to consider in what medium of culture I might do such modest theological work as lay within my scope, I

---

* Numbers refer to notes, which will be found, arranged by chapters, beginning on page 117.

could not resist the feeling that the real nub of the matter, so far as the self-interpretation of man in our period goes, is to be found in the great literature of our time. Here, it seemed, was "the richest mine of confessional experience and spiritual exploration . . . available since the Renaissance." [5] And I have remained steadfast in my conviction that, outside theology itself, the literary intelligence is by far the best intelligence of our time, better than the philosophic intelligence, better than the social-scientific intelligence, and better perhaps even, on the whole, than the theological. For the great writers of the modern period—say, Joyce and Lawrence and Kafka and Eliot and Auden, to mention only a few—seem to have traveled farther than most of the rest of us and seem to have thrust us more exactly upon the centers of our distress than any other class of modern thinkers has succeeded in doing. This is by no means to say that they have not often erred. In venturing out into the exposed and uncharted paths that await the human pilgrim in our day they have, to be sure, sometimes stumbled in the darkness and fallen on the devious terrain and suffered the hurts that pioneers of new ways of feeling and thinking must endure. But the great thing is that they have *ventured:* when they have recommended a route into hope and health, it may not always have been the right one, but at least they convince us that they have not evaded "the stricken weathers" of our moment in history; and thus it is possible for us to feel that the stage on which their dramas are enacted is a map of the modern psyche.

So, among the major departments of modern cultural life, that by which, as a theologian, my own imagination came to be most deeply engaged was the realm of poetry and drama and the novel. And, as a consequence, much of what I have focused upon over the past dozen years or so has involved an effort to discover ways of bringing the literature of our period to "the level of religious emergence," [6] where it may be apprehended as "testimony" and as the vehicle of the "ultimate concerns" which define the spiritual situation of our age. The order of what has been my progress is accurately reflected in the arrangement of the chapters of this book, for I had first of all to seek a usable historical perspective upon what have actually been the relations between poetry and religion in the modern period (Chapter I); then I had to enter into a dialogue with the custodians in modern criticism of the literary tradition (Chapter II) in order to discover what my own theological position might entail with respect to some of the major issues in theory of literature; next, I had to undertake, tentatively, to define in constructive terms a body of principle by which the Christian reader may be guided in his transactions with literary art (Chapter III); and, finally, I wanted to look at the rich and highly diversified body of literature that presses in upon us in our own time (Chapters IV, V, and VI), by way of working toward a definition of the reports and prophecies that it offers as a summary of the modern consciousness.

I cannot begin, in this Preface, really to catalogue the indebtments that I have incurred. The notes will, of course, indicate some of the volumes on my shelves that are most dog-eared, but my reflections have also been influenced by a few friends whose identity is nowhere revealed in any of my notes. During our years together as students in Ann Arbor in the early 'forties (where he was then in the Graduate School of the University and I was an undergraduate), my good friend, the poet Robert Hayden (of Fisk University), though he may now have forgotten it, was responsible for many of my first discoveries in modern literature. And, late in the 'forties, another friend, Clinton Oliver, had a share in my education, though, again, he too may now have forgotten this: he had been a student of Matthiessen's at Harvard and had the kind of profound understanding of our American tradition in literature that all of Matthiessen's best students have and that I needed greatly to profit from; indeed, it was he who was responsible for my first reading *American Renaissance* and for my first really serious reading of Henry James and of many contemporaries. And in recent times conversations with my friend and colleague Preston Roberts have often greatly helped me to find my way amongst the complex dimensions of the task that confronts the literary critic in our day who takes his moorings in a theological orientation.

I must also express here a word of thanks to my "chief," Dean Jerald Brauer of the Federated Theological Faculty of the University of Chicago, who, in releasing me from my teaching duties during the Spring Quarter of 1957, provided me with a period of relative leisure, a portion of which was used to prepare these pages for the press.

And, of course, apart from my wife Charlotte neither life nor study would bring happiness and fulfillment: she remains, as I have said in another Preface, the loyal partner and very "heart of grace" without whom nothing would be accomplished at all.

N. A. S., Jr.

The Federated Theological Faculty
The University of Chicago
March 26, 1958

Acknowledgments

Since the growth of this book is something that has occurred in public, I must express my gratitude here to the audiences and the editors who, at various stages along the way, provided me with a platform. The third chapter was originally delivered in the form of two public lectures at the University of Chicago in April of 1955, under the sponsorship of the University's Federated Theological Faculty; and it was subsequently published under its present title in *The Journal of Religion* (Vol. XXXV, No. 4, October, 1955). The second chapter grows out of a paper ("The Collaboration of Vision in the Poetic Act: Its Establishment of the Religious Dimension," published in *Cross Currents,* Vol. VII, No. 2, Spring, 1957) that was read before the English Institute at Columbia University in September of 1956 and, also, an essay on "The Relation of Theology to Literary Criticism" that appeared in *The Journal of Religion* (Vol. XXXIII, No. 4, October, 1953). This latter essay, together with the first chapter and some of the materials in the fourth chapter, formed the basis of three lectures that were delivered before a faculty conference of the Student Christian Movement in New England in East Northfield, Massachusetts, in January of 1953; and the same lectures were presented at Columbia University in March of 1953 under the sponsorship of the Protestant Graduate and Faculty Group. A portion of the third chapter also formed the basis of a lecture delivered in January of 1953 before a senior seminar in "Great Issues" at Fisk University and before the Institute of Religious and Social Studies of the Jewish Theological Seminary of America in New York City. Then, subsequent to the delivery of these lectures, the first chapter appeared under its present title in *The Journal of Religion* (Vol. XXXIII, No. 3, July, 1953), and a large part of the fourth chapter appeared as an essay (under the title "Religious Symbolism in Contemporary Literature") in the volume *Religious Symbolism,* edited by F. Ernest Johnson (New York: Institute for Religious and Social Studies, Harper & Brothers, 1955). A portion of the fifth chapter formed the basis of a lecture delivered at the McCormick Theological Seminary in Chicago, at Knox College in Galesburg, Illinois, and at the Lutheran Theological Seminary in Gettysburg, Pennsylvania, in March, April, and May of 1957; another part of this chapter was written earlier for delivery as a lecture in a series on "The Arts and Protestant Culture" at the Judson Memorial Church in New York City in March of 1955 and was published in *Motive* under the title "The Personal Principle in Recent Literature and Its Religious Implication" (Vol. XV, No. 8, May, 1955); still another part of this chapter appeared in an article entitled "A Kingdom Foreseen: An Assessment of Contemporary Literature" that was published in *The Intercollegian* (Vol. 71, No. 2, October, 1953). One part of the sixth chapter appeared under the present title in *Christianity and Crisis* (Vol. XVI, No. 16, October 1, 1956), and another portion of this chapter appeared as an article entitled "Poetry and Religion: A Relation Reconsidered" in *The Chicago Theological Seminary Register* (Vol. XLVI, No. 1, January, 1956). Other materials are drawn from an article that appeared in *The Intercollegian* under the title "The Testimony of the Novel" (Vol. 69, No. 8, April, 1952). A brief passage in Chapter V is drawn from my review of Gabriel Marcel's Gifford Lectures in *The Journal of Religious Thought,* Vol. XII, No. 1 (Autumn-Winter, 1954–55).

The second chapter is also scheduled to appear in a forthcoming volume of essays dealing with theology and literary criticism being edited by Professor Preston T. Roberts, Jr., of the University of Chicago.

Previously published materials are used here with the permission of the editors in whose journals they appeared; and thanks are also given to the Institute for Religious and Social Studies for permitting the use of materials that originally appeared in their symposium on *Religious Symbolism,* edited by F. Ernest Johnson.

The author is indebted to the following publishers for permission to use quotations from volumes of poetry for which they hold the copyrights: Random House (Karl Shapiro, *Essay on Rime,* originally published by Reynal and Hitchcock; W. H. Auden, *The Collected Poetry*), the Noonday Press (Louise Bogan, *The Sleeping Fury,* originally published by Charles Scribner's Sons), Harcourt, Brace and Co. and Faber and Faber Ltd. (T. S. Eliot, *Four Quartets* and *Family Reunion*).

Modern Literature and the Religious Frontier

Poetry, Religion, and the Modern Mind

THE NOTION IS worth entertaining, I believe, that the prevailing conception of the proper uses of language provides the most revealing clue to the state of health of a people's culture. For the possession of meaning involves the possession of words, and to know the uses to which men believe words may be put is to have a deep insight into the dimensions of meaning which their culture is capable of assimilating. We might, indeed, move one step further and say that when men begin to make their language the object of radical scrutiny and deliberate legislation, they betray their profound anxiety about the social and cultural vitality of the commonwealth to which they belong. To view our own culture, at any rate, from this standpoint is to be confronted by the deep illness of our age.

That illness may be defined in terms of the belief, pervasive throughout our period, that the whole of experience may be subsumed under the categories of empirical science—a belief which is accompanied by a consequent impatience with those elements of our experience that resist such disposal. It has, indeed, become the habit of our contemporaries to be chronically uneasy before what with a certain distrust they call subjectivity—that is, the spiritual, the internal, all those subtle modulations and resonances of the human story that cannot be flattened out into the equations of the natural and social sciences. Surely it is this general state of mind, for example, that provides the explanation of the phenomenal reception that a few years ago was accorded what has come to be known as "The Kinsey Report." [1] The uncritical enthusiasm with which the appearance of that document was hailed by great numbers of intelligent men and women proceeded, I am convinced, from their satisfaction with its physicalistic procedure of separating the sexual life from the total psychic structure, with its tacit suggestion that the entire range of man's sexuality may be described in purely anatomical and physiological terms. The Report's tendency to regard the sexual experience as totally comprised by the physical act, and its adoption of purely quantitative principles of evidence, doubtless appeared to the American public to confirm their own indisposition to involve themselves with all those "ideas that do not seem to be, as it were, immediately dictated by simple physical fact." [2] The cultural event, in other words, that was constituted by the Report's reception—unprecedentedly extensive for a scientific treatise—signalized the deep aversion in our period to ideas and modes of apprehending the human situation that are not easily reducible to the terms of positivist procedure.

The historical crisis of our time in which the moral neutrality of science has been so terrifyingly revealed has, of course, begun to force our generation to wonder whether, after all, there are not other approaches to truth besides those provided by the observational and experimental techniques of science. And philosophy, which most educated men of secular orientation tend to regard as the custodian of the traditional humanistic disciplines, has therefore again come to have a kind of ambiguous dignity in our cultural life today. The irony of the present situation, however, is that modern philosophy has no such platform as did nineteenth-century Idealism from which any truly subversive critical program might be directed against the positivistic nominalism that has become so deeply ingrained in that part of our culture where assumption rules. Recent developments in academic philosophy represent very largely a most unfortunate surrender to that tendency, and our most influential schoolmen today, in fact, call themselves logical positivists or, sometimes, scientific empiricists. So, at a time when "thinking men and women . . . are exclaiming that, while science has made sufficient advance to satisfy all our material needs, what we most need, and must find if we are not to suffer shipwreck, is a new sense of values, a new religious awakening and a new orientation towards life, in short, a new philosophy" [3]—at a time when this is coming more and more to be the general testimony, it turns out that our most advanced philosophers have become "the dogmatic theologians and heresiologists of the Orthodox Church of Natural Science." [4] In this role they assure us that it is the business of philosophy not to study experience but rather to study the logical structure of sentences, particularly of those sentences which have to do with the structural relationships between actual sense data, since the knowledge of the basic structure of nature is the only kind of knowledge that is possible for man. Man may have other desires and needs besides those which are satisfied by scientific knowledge, these philosophers tell us—such cravings as are ministered to by art and religion—but the myths which he fashions to satisfy these requirements of his nature have significance only in the private world of individual subjectivity. And the private world of individual subjectivity exists outside of that public world described by science upon which meaningful discussion may alone be based, since it is of this world alone that we can have genuine knowledge. The well-known popularizer in this area of study, Mr. Lancelot Hogben, remarks, for example: "So soon as we engage in public discourse we are compelled to seek for a neutral ground. We agree to leave our private world behind. To make discourse possible we accept this neutral ground as the real thing. This neutral ground," he says, "is the public world of science." [5] And we assume that he means to tell us that, apart from the world which is the object of scientific study, intelligible discourse is impossible.

Mr. Hogben echoes at this point a school of thought in modern philosophy that takes its origin, on the one hand, from British philosophers like G. E. Moore and Bertrand Russell and, on the other hand, from Continental thinkers like that brilliantly eccentric figure, the late Ludwig Wittgenstein, and his colleagues in the so-called "Vienna Circle" of Schlick and Carnap and Neurath. And their progeny on the contemporary scene include men like A. J. Ayer in Britain and C. L. Stevenson in this country and most of the young people who teach philosophy today in our universities. For this whole modern movement, philosophy and theology and poetry are all "a kind of mental cramp produced by linguistic disorder" [6]—a disorder growing out of our failure to employ a consistently univocal speech which represents, these men believe, the only valid use of language. And, indeed, when the highly intricate subtleties of their doctrine are reduced to their final implication, it does appear that the positivists are talking, fundamentally, about the problem of language and are distinguishing between what they consider to be its two main uses. On the one hand, they tell us, we may speak scientifically or referentially, and to speak in this manner is to speak sensibly; or, on the other hand, we may speak emotively or homiletically, and to speak in this manner is to spout nonsense. Their point is that scientific or referential statements are meaningful because they are verifiable: they propose, that is to say, assertions about sense data, the accuracy of which may be checked by empirical observation. If I were to say, for example, that in the 1600 block of Pennsylvania Avenue in the District of Columbia there is a building called the White House in which the President of our country resides, I should be speaking sensibly, so the positivists would argue, for anyone who cared to go to Washington and make the proper investigations could easily verify the truthfulness of my statement. But for Mr. T. S. Eliot to declare, for example, as he does in "The Love Song of J. Alfred Prufrock," that "the evening is spread out against the sky/Like a patient etherised upon a table"—for Mr. Eliot to speak in this way is for him to put forward a statement with which the grammarian cannot deal, since it is an example of what Mr. I. A. Richards in his early book *Science and Poetry* called a "pseudo-statement," that is, a statement which designates a state of affairs whose existence cannot be empirically established. Or, again, if Mr. Cleanth Brooks, let us say, were to argue that Mr. Eliot's poem is a better poem than *The Hamlet* of Archibald MacLeish or if M. Jacques Maritain were to argue for the existence of God, they would both be told that they were speaking emotively and therefore nonsensically. Mr. Brooks would perhaps be reminded by Mr. Ayer that "one really never does dispute about questions of value," [7] and M. Maritain would be told that metaphysical and theological sentences, though they purport to express genuine propositions, actually express neither tautologies nor empirical hypotheses. "And as tautologies and empirical hypotheses form the entire class of significant propositions," Mr. Ayer would say, "we are justified in concluding that all metaphysical assertions are nonsensical." [8] The nonsense of Messrs. Brooks and Maritain might not be altogether useless, Mr. Ayer would admit, for through it they might express their feelings and might even succeed in changing other people's feelings; but their language would patently not be of the sort whose truthfulness could be fruitfully discussed: at best, their respective disciplines could be regarded only as abortive proliferations of psychology and sociology. But they, of course, might perhaps be forgiven for regarding Mr. Ayer's *a priori* settlement of the matter as somewhat highhanded.

What it is of some interest, though, for us to observe at this point is that the high priests of the new orthodoxy in modern philosophy concur with the greatest of the pagan philosophers—for reasons, however, which are theirs and not his—in believing that poetry must be banished from the Just City, and not poetry alone, they say, but metaphysics and theology as well. And this suggests to us, therefore, that perhaps, at least in the context of the contemporary intellectual situation, these departments of our culture have a more than tangential relationship to one another. So it is by no means inappropriate that those of us who are today concerned about the future of religion should at the same time be concerned about the future of poetry and should seek to defend them both against a certain fashionable and sophisticated barbarism in our own time that would regard them both as being, in Mr. Arthur Mizener's phrase, "amiable insanity."

Now the relation of imaginative literature to religion, or theology, is greatly clarified when we remember that the disparagement of their cognitive seriousness is a strain in modern culture that antedates by at least three hundred years the neopositivism of Wittgenstein's *Tractatus,* of *The International Encyclopedia of Unified Science,* and Mr. Ayer's *Language, Truth and Logic.* Indeed, a main segment of contemporary criticism has been devoted to the insistence that in order fully to understand the modern divorce between intellect and imagination, between sense and sensibility, we must go back to the seventeenth century. Mr. Herbert Muller says that we should go back to the empiricism of Johannes Kepler.[9] Mr. Basil Willey feels that Descartes's disjunction of "mind" and "matter" is the point at which historical analysis of these matters should begin,[10] and Mr. L. C. Knights directs us back to Francis Bacon.[11] My own feeling is that Hobbes, if not perhaps an ultimate source of the modern "dissociation of sensibility," at least provides us with highly relevant evidence of the roots from which many of our cultural predicaments are sprung. Perhaps it is true that Descartes's division of reality into thought and extension, his doctrinaire claim of a superior status in reality for those things which may be weighed and measured, and his assumption that the denotative language of mathematics is the clearest language and therefore the surest way of arriving at truth—perhaps it is true that his main legacy was hostile to both religion and poetry and consequently "reinforced the growing disposition to accept the scientific world-picture as the only 'true' one." [12] Perhaps it is also true that Bacon, in his role as propagandist, greatly advanced the whole program of modern scientific rationalism and that he too was a primary directive force. But I suspect that it is from Hobbes that we most directly inherit much of the tension in modern culture between the intellect and the imagination. And his modernity nowhere shows itself more plainly than in his concern with the problem of language—which is the chief interest of contemporary philosophy—and his extreme nominalism relates him directly to our neopositivistic semanticists, to men like C. K. Ogden and I. A. Richards and Charles W. Morris.

Hobbes belonged, of course, to an age the progress of whose thought was to reveal, increasingly as it unfolded, the irony of late scholasticism. Ockham, for example, when he insisted upon the independence of theology from reasoning based upon evidence of the senses, had done so not for the sake of thereby making theology irrelevant to the pursuit of truth but in order to establish it more securely upon the basis of its unique procedures—between which and those of the experimental sciences he could conceive of no serious conflict. He believed, as did the nominalists generally, that there were truths of nature and truths of spirit, that both had their validity, and that there need be no unfriendly struggle between them. But, then, by the advent of the seventeenth century the ideologues of the new science had lost Ockham's conviction that science must be the handmaid of religion and, having become more interested in the world of nature than in anything else, could use his separation of religion from science to dispose of it altogether.

The materialism of Hobbes was, in other words, an inevitable development of his period, and it gains its most succinct statement in the forty-sixth chapter of the *Leviathan,* where he says:

> The *Universe,* that is, the whole masse of all things that are, is Corporeall, that is to say, Body; and hath the dimensions of Magnitude, namely, Length, Bredth, and Depth: also every part of the Body, is likewise Body, and hath the like dimensions; and consequently every part of the Universe, is Body; and that which is not Body, is no part of the Universe: And because the Universe is All, that which is no part of it, is Nothing; and consequently *no where.*

Matter, that is to say, was for him the final reality—the ultimately irreducible particles which occupy space and which make themselves known to the human percipient "by the pressure, that is by the motion, of externall things upon our Eyes, Eares, and other organs thereunto ordained." Only those perceptions which come to us through the external senses are real, and language is therefore properly used only when it is employed for the presentation of the evidences of sensory experience and of the material reality which that experience conveys. Indeed, he leaves us in no doubt at all as to what his intention is. He says:

> Speciall uses of speech are these, First, to Register, what by cogitation,

wee find to be the cause of any thing, present or past; and what we find things present or past may produce, or effect: which in summe, is acquiring of Arts, Secondly, to shew to others that knowledge which we have attained; which is, to Counsell, and Teach one another. Thirdly, to make known to others our wills, and purposes, that we may have the mutuall help of one another. Fourthly, to please and delight our selves, and others, by playing with our words, for pleasure or ornament, innocently.

To these Uses, there are also foure correspondent Abuses. First, when men register their thoughts wrong, by the inconstancy of the signification of their words; by which they register for their conceptions, that which they never conceived; and so deceive themselves. Secondly, when they use words metaphorically; that is, in other sense than that they are ordained for; and thereby deceive others. Thirdly, when by words they declare that to be their will, which is not. Fourthly, when they use them to grieve one another. . . .

What Hobbes wanted was a plain, straightforward language purged of all the rich ambiguity of Elizabethan and Jacobean diction—the kind of language that Thomas Sprat in his *History of the Royal Society* (1667) called "a close, naked, natural way of speaking . . . bringing all things as near the Mathematical plainness as they can. . . ." And these canons could be satisfied neither by the language of poetry nor by the language of religion. Poetry was, in his view, sheer frivolity —though religion could be admitted on tolerance into his Commonwealth, since it might serve as a guarantor of civil peace and order. Both, however, were to be distrusted, since theirs is, characteristically, a language that is riddled with metaphor and analogy and that fails therefore of the kind of univocal clarity that Hobbes considered essential for all serious and responsible discourse. Words, he believed, may be properly used only to designate real things and the connections between real things—according, of course, to his own criterion of reality that was based upon the scientific materialism of Galileo. And all other uses of speech may "please and delight our selves, and others . . . innocently," but they will ultimately deceive and lead to absurdity.

Hobbes's segregation of the symbolic, of the metaphorical and the analogical, from serious discourse is revealed most plainly in his theories of Fancy and Judgment. This phase of his thought is extremely confused, and it is often very difficult to detect consistency. The chief source of the obscurity is what appears to be his desire at times simply to define Fancy as the act of the mind whereby "unexpected similitude" is discerned in "things otherwise much unlike" and to define Judgment as the act of finding dissimilitude in things that are identical. And, so defined, Fancy and Judgment make up what is called Wit. But one feels that his deeper instinct is to contrast Fancy and Judgment in such a way as to make Fancy represent extravagant indiscretion, the kind of undisciplined vivacity of mind whereby the contents of the memory are quickly reviewed and superficially congruous ideas combined to make pleasant pictures and pretty images, while Judgment is serious intellectual discernment and therefore quite different from the frivolous gaiety of Fancy. However pleasant and pretty, though, the constructions of Fancy may be, it will not be assumed, Hobbes took for granted, that they are conformable to truth and reason. For "truth" is the possession of Judgment and of reason and is often to be had only after the mind has disabused itself of those phantasms which are the creations of Fancy. Fancy, the faculty of the mind which is operative in poetic and religious experience, is, in other words, a principle of triviality, and the "emotive" language through which it articulates itself, though it may "please and delight our selves, and others," is incapable of giving a responsible version of experience.

This, then, was the main legacy which Hobbes bequeathed to the chief theorists of neoclassicism, to Dryden, to Locke and Addison, to Hume and Reynolds—and even as late as Wordsworth and Coleridge the doctrines of Fancy and of Judgment, in the modified form of the Fancy-Imagination distinction, are still playing an important role in English poetics. The distinction could, of course, be maintained, as Mr. Basil Willey has said, only by generations who had been taught to believe that "the fact-world of modern scientific consciousness was the primary datum" [13] and who were the inheritors of a tradition which, stemming from Hobbes, "stood for common sense and naturalism, and the monopoly of the scientific spirit over the mind." [14] The poet had been given to understand, as Locke put it in the *Essay concerning Human Understanding,* that all he had to offer were "pleasant pictures and agreeable visions," and, however attractive these might be, he was assured that they consisted in nothing "perfectly conformable" to truth and reason. Poetry had "been reduced . . . to providing embellishments which might be agreeable to the fancy, but which were recognized by the judgment as having no relation to 'reality.' " [15] And as both religion and poetry sprang from quite other modes of knowing than the faculty designated by neoclassical theory as "judgment," the result was that religion sank to deism and poetry was "reduced to catering for 'delight' " [16] or to making the effort to conform with truth and reason. So, on the one hand, one comes upon men like Locke and Shaftesbury and Butler and Hume, who were intent upon establishing the existence of a purely verbal God and who were making of theology little more than "an arbitrary code of morals and a pseudo-science of entities which cannot be known through the senses." [17] While the poets, having been told by Hobbes and Locke that they could not trust what they *felt* (Fancy) as human beings or as poets but only what they *thought* as men of sense and Judgment, were avoiding the bold metaphors and drastic ironies of the school of Donne and subjecting their language to the sobrieties of the barest denotation in the manner of Pope's *Essay on Man*. Or, if they were not producing a poetry of *thought,* they were producing a poetry of *feeling* in "conscious disregard of contemporary truth-standards" [18] in the manner of Gray's *Odes*. But in any event we may hold Hobbes responsible in large part, as Mr. John Crowe Ransom has suggested, for "the chill" [19] which settled upon both poetry and religion in the century that followed—a condition that Mr. Eliot has covered in his famous phrase "dissociation of sensibility." [20]

Now it is a commonplace of the school textbooks that by the last decade of the eighteenth century a reaction against neoclassicism had set in, the principal documents of which we may regard as being Wordsworth's Preface to the *Lyrical Ballads* and Coleridge's *Biographia Literaria*. And the main object of the Romantic revolt against the eighteenth century we may define as having been that of rescuing the doctrine of the imagination from the desuetude into which it had fallen in the hands of neoclassical theorists. For a century English thought had been dominated by the materialism of Hobbes and the sensationalism of Locke, which had served neither poetry nor religion well, because, the Romantics believed, the world described by Hobbes and Locke is not a world susceptible of imaginative prehension. Locke's Deity was, of course, "that of the eighteenth century as a whole—a Deity to be approached by demonstration, and whose existence, proclaimed by the spacious firmament on high, is as well attested as any proof in Euclid." [21] And though he regarded the imagination, or rather what he and Hobbes called Wit, as being the constitutive principle of poetry, he could approve of it only in so far as it was controlled by Judgment, a principle which he defined in the *Essay concerning Human Understanding* in such a way as to leave us in no doubt at all as to his sense of its extreme opposition to Wit. "This," he says, is a way of proceeding quite contrary to metaphor and allusion, wherein for the most part lies that *entertainment and pleasantry of wit* which strikes so lively on the fancy, and therefore so acceptable to all people, because its beauty appears at first sight, and there is required *no labour of thought to examine what truth or reason there is in it.*

Implicit in his entire understanding of both poetry and religion, in other words, was the assumption that the "inanimate cold world" of mechanistic materialism constituted the whole of reality. And though a kind of attenuated religion and the kind of literature produced by the contemporaries of Dryden, Pope, and Johnson could maintain themselves on such a basis, the Romantics believed it to be in principle hostile to every aspect of the spiritual life. We are not, they said, wholly passive recipients in the process of perception, mere registrants of impressions from the external world without, as Locke had contended. Nor is the world itself simply a system of matter organized along the lines of mechanism; it is, fundamentally, they felt, a universe of spirit whose glory and mystery are more deeply to be grasped by the imagination than by the analytical reason. So, Coleridge concluded: "If the mind be not *passive,* if it be indeed made in God's image, and that, too, in the sublimest sense, the *Image of the Creator,* there is ground for the suspicion that any system built on the passiveness of the mind must be false as a system." [22]

Though some of the Romantics—Blake, for example, and Keats perhaps—were not so philosophically sophisticated as Coleridge and did not perhaps even share his philosophical preoccupations, they were all profoundly at odds, whether consciously so or not, with the sensationalist view of the world; and they were at one with each other in their belief in the primacy of the imagination. The basic article of their creed was given by Coleridge when he declared: "The primary imagination I hold to be the living Power and prime Agent of all human Perception, and as a repetition in the finite mind of the eternal act of creation in the infinite *I am.*" [23] And on another occasion he remarked: "Imagination is possibly in man a lesser degree of the creative power of God." [24]

Now it is essential that we remember that Blake and Coleridge and Wordsworth and Shelley apotheosized the imagination in the name of an ulterior reality and a transcendental truth to which they believed it alone gave sure access. They were, in fact, possessed by a sense of the *numinous,* and it was the habit of their natures to utter an *o altitudo* in the presence of what Rudolf Otto in our own time called the *mysterium tremendum*. Indeed, as Professor C. M. Bowra has said:

> The Romantic movement was a prodigious attempt to discover the world of spirit through the unaided efforts of the solitary soul. It was a special manifestation of that belief in the worth of the individual which philosophers and politicians had recently preached to the world.[25]

Their insistence upon the imagination was, in other words, determined by their conviction that it must be related to truth and reality and that it alone could give transport to the world beyond. The Romantic "Imagination," that is to say, was not the neoclassical "Fancy": it was, in fact, distinguished quite as sharply from "Fancy" as, in neoclassical theory, "Judgment" had been set apart from "Wit." And Wordsworth and Coleridge would have concurred with Ruskin, who was much later to declare in the second volume of *Modern Painters:* "There is in every word set down by the imaginative mind an awful undercurrent of meaning, and evidence and shadow upon it of the deep places out of which it has come. . . . Imagination cannot but be serious; she sees too far, too darkly, too solemnly, too earnestly, ever to smile."

So the highest office of poetry is not that of generating chimeras and fictions; on the contrary, the poet, "deeply drinking-in the soul of things," penetrates to their melancholy depths and gives us a directive wisdom. Which had, of course, in a way, been the contention of Hobbes and Locke, and thus Mr. Cleanth Brooks is justified, I believe, in making the point that the Romantic revolt actually altered very little the prime essential of neoclassical poetics. For whereas Hobbes and the members of the Royal Society were willing to tolerate the poet so long as he discussed in a logically decorous way with his contemporaries the principles of mechanico-materialism, Wordsworth and Coleridge could, on the other hand, approve only of the poet who, as an oracle of a transcendent reality, sought to "disimprison the soul of fact" and give a vision of the Absolute, to "incite and to support the eternal." By both schools the poet is viewed primarily as a serious expositor who, in forgoing the abrupt conceits and daring imagery of Fancy, seeks to achieve what Dr. Johnson called "the grandeur of generality." And so we should, therefore, not find surprising the reservations which both schools had about the metaphysical poets of the early seventeenth century and which, were their chief spokesmen to be miraculously resurrected today, they would doubtless have about much that has happened in modern poetry since Mr. Eliot spoke of the evening "spread out against the sky/Like a patient etherised upon a table."

Mr. Archibald MacLeish's dictum in our own time, "A poem should not mean/But be," could not, one suspects, have easily gained acceptance by the Romantics, for to them poetry was that superior activity of mind—"Reason in her most exalted mood"—whereby Truth in its loveliest and most ultimate forms may be apprehended. And, in this as in many other respects, it is Shelley who provides us with what is perhaps most nearly a normative expression of the Romantic mind. The document which I have in mind is his *Defense of Poetry,* in which he begins by distinguishing between "two classes of mental action, which are called reason and imagination." Reason, he says, is the "principle of analysis, and its action regards the relation of things, simply as relations; considering thoughts, not in their integral unity, but as the algebraical representations which conduct to certain general results." Imagination, on the other hand, is "the principle of synthesis, and has for its object those forms which are common to universal nature and existence itself." "Reason is the enumeration of quantities already known; imagination is the perception of the value of those quantities, both separately and as a whole."

Shelley goes on to argue that "poetry, in a general sense, may be defined as 'the expression of the imagination'" and that "a poem is the image of life expressed in its eternal truth." The art of poetry is an art of divination: "A poet," he says, "participates in the eternal, the infinite, and the one." He is a seer and a priest who mediates to the human community that indestructible spiritual order which is dimly glimpsed in the "partial apprehension of the agencies of the invisible world which is called religion." He "defeats the curse which binds us" to the phenomenal world and "redeems from decay the visitations of the divinity in man." Shelley says:

Poetry turns all things to loveliness; it exalts the beauty of that which is most beautiful, and it adds beauty to that which is most deformed; it marries exultation and horror, grief and pleasure, eternity and change; it subdues to union, under its light yoke, all irreconcilable things. It transmutes all that it touches, and every form moving within the radiance of its presence is changed by wondrous sympathy to an incarnation of the spirit which it breathes.

So it is our best hope of a better world:

The most unfailing herald, companion, and follower of the awakening of a great people to work a beneficial change in opinion or institution, is Poetry. . . . Poets are the hierophants of an unapprehended inspiration; the mirrors of the gigantic shadows which futurity casts upon the present; the words which express what they understand not; the trumpets which sing to battle, and feel not what they inspire; the influence which is moved not, but moves. Poets are the unacknowledged legislators of the world.

Shelley provides us, then, with an extreme example of the wooziness in which the Romantics, in their theoretical moments, often came to be bogged down: it is what T. E. Hulme called their "spilt religion," their predilection for creating their metaphysics and theology out of their poetic experience rather than formulating poetic attitudes on the basis of metaphysical-theological principles. The ironical result, in other words, of their effort to rescue the imagination, in both its aesthetic and religious phases, from neoclassical rationalism turns out to be a further sentimentalization of religion and a general debilitation of poetry.

From Shelley, at the beginning of the nineteenth century, and his confusion of poetic and religious experience it is but a step to Matthew Arnold's disquisitions on poetry and the higher seriousness in the latter half of the century, though the author of "The Study of Poetry" more nearly takes his moorings in Wordsworth than in Shelley. With Arnold the effort of a department of the modern mind to defend itself against the attacks of positivism and science achieves the completion of a result already foreshadowed in the Romantics—namely, the usurpation by poetry of the place of religion. And, when Arnold assures us that religion is nothing more than "morality touched by emotion," he again brings to a point of culmination the tendency of the Romantics "to leave Religion to be laid waste by the anarchy of feeling." [26] The language of *God and the Bible* clearly indicates that he could not regard it as any longer possible for a man of intelligence to hold seriously any orthodox version of Christianity; its assertions, he says,

. . . have convinced no one, they have given rest to no one, they have given joy to no one. People have swallowed them, people have fought over them, people have shown their ingenuity over them; but no one has ever enjoyed them. Nay, no one has ever really understood them.

But, in the very first paragraph of "The Study of Poetry," he tells us:

The future of poetry is immense, because in poetry, where it is worthy of its high destinies, our race, as time goes on, will find an ever surer and surer stay. There is not a creed which is not shaken, not an accredited dogma which is not shown to be questionable, not a received tradition which does not threaten to dissolve. Our religion has materialized itself in the fact, in the supposed fact; it has attached its emotion to the fact, and now the fact is failing it. But for poetry the idea is everything; the rest is a world of illusion, of divine illusion. Poetry attaches its emotion to the idea; the idea *is* the fact. The strongest part of our religion today is its unconscious poetry.

So, farther on in the essay, he declares:

More and more mankind will discover that we have to turn to poetry to interpret life for us, to console us, to sustain us. Without poetry, our science will appear incomplete and most of what now passes with us for religion and philosophy will be replaced by poetry.

To speak of Arnold is, of course, to be brought back into our own immediate time, for, as Mr. Eliot remarked many years ago in his Norton Lectures, "we are still in the Arnold period"; [27] and, as he has also said, were Arnold to be resurrected in the contemporary world, he would have his work to do over again. Arnold's problem—which still is ours—might be said to have been essentially that of the Romantic generations before him, of somehow vindicating the claims of the imagination against the contrary claims of modern scientific positivism. And his way of dealing with that problem was to give up the ghost so far as religion was concerned and to grant the impossibility of its continued maintenance in any form continuous with historic Christian orthodoxy. Religion could, in the modern world, be regarded only as "morality touched with emotion," and it was imaginative literature, Arnold believed, that could best "touch conduct with emotion." So literature, like science, was to be valued as an aid in the practical mastery of the world, as a kind of descriptive science, dealing with that level of experience which is touched with emotion. And so viewed, he declared, its future "is immense."

The most famous advocate of this view of our subject in contemporary discussion has been Mr. I. A. Richards—or, as one must perhaps now say, the "early" Richards, since the more recent phase of his development, first signalized by *Coleridge on Imagination,* seems to represent a considerable modification of the position which he earlier formulated in such books as *The Meaning of Meaning, The Principles of Literary Criticism, Practical Criticism,* and *Science and Poetry.* The early Richards, however, was much more strict in his logic than was Arnold. For, though he too regarded poetic language as being essentially a rhetorical vehicle of ideas, he did not share Arnold's supposition that it could live in honorable peace with the rhetoric of science. The author of *Science and Poetry* was, of course, a positivist who held that view of language which I outlined earlier, in accordance with which it is argued that language may be used either emotively or referentially —the former characterizing poetic and religious discourse, the latter characterizing scientific discourse. Mr. Richards's way of putting this was to say that poetry is constituted of "pseudo-statements" whose truth claims cannot successfully rival those of the "certified scientific state- ments" of technical discourse. But why, then, one wonders, if this is the case, should poetry be tolerated at all? The answer to this question may be found in his total outlook, which in 1926, the year that *Science and Poetry* appeared, was a hodgepodge of philosophical materialism and ethical utilitarianism, at the base of which lay a theory of value that was derived from psychological behaviorism. He regarded the mind as a system of impulses or "interests," each one of which contends with all the others for the mastery. Here, for example, is a central passage from *Science and Poetry:*

Suppose that we carry a magnetic compass about in the neighbourhood of powerful magnets. The needle waggles as we move and comes to rest pointing in a new direction whenever we stand still in a new position. Sup- pose that instead of a single compass we carry an arrangement of many magnetic needles, large and small, swung so that they influence one an- other, some able only to swing horizontally, others vertically, others hung freely. As we move, the perturbations in this system will be very compli- cated. But for every position in which we place it there will be a final posi- tion of rest for all the needles into which they will in the end settle down, a general poise for the whole system. But even a slight displacement may set the whole assemblage of needles busily readjusting themselves.

One further complication. Suppose that while all the needles influence one another, some of them respond only to some of the outer magnets among which the system is moving. The reader can easily draw a diagram if his imagination needs a visual support.

The mind is not unlike such a system if we imagine it to be incredibly complex. The needles are our interests, varying in their importance, that is in the degree to which any movement they make involves movement in the other needles. Each new disequilibrium, which a shift of position, a fresh situation, entails, corresponds to a need: and the wagglings which ensue as the system rearranges itself are our responses, the impulses through which we seek to meet the need.

Now it is impossible for all our needs and interests to be gratified, but those things are to be valued most highly, Mr. Richards argued, which satisfy the greatest number of our desires in the least wasteful manner—that is, "with as little conflict, as little mutual interference between different subsystems" of our activities, as there need be. And if one asks what it feels like to achieve this maximal satisfaction of interests, Mr. Richards's answer was simply that "it feels like and is the experience of poetry."

The way of poetry is not the only way of dealing with the tensions arising in the human psyche out of conflicts between "appetencies." These conflicts may be dealt with either by way of "conquest" or by way of "conciliation." But the way of conquest, whatever may be the attractiveness of Stoicism, is not to be recommended, for, he says:

> People who are always winning victories over themselves might equally well be described as always enslaving themselves. Their lives become unnecessarily narrow. The minds of many saints have been like wells; they should have been like lakes or like the sea.

The way of conquest does not, in other words, result in that organization of our interests which is least wasteful of human possibilities. The better way, therefore, is the way of "conciliation," and this is the way of poetry. For poetry, we must remember, is constituted of "pseudo-statements," and Mr. Richards's definition of a "pseudo-statement" was this: "a form of words which is justified entirely by its effect in releasing or organizing our impulses and attitudes (due regard being had for the better or worse organizations of these *inter se*)." "The artist," he said, "is concerned with the record and perpetuation of the experiences which seem to him most worth having. . . . He is the point at which the growth of the mind shows itself. . . . His work is the ordering of what in most minds is disordered."

This, then, I take it, is the meaning that lay behind Mr. Richards's now famous declaration that "poetry is capable of saving us." But, when he made this declaration, he did not at all mean to deny that poetry is, nevertheless, nonsense. For his criterion of meaning was a positivist criterion, and in reply to Hart Crane's remark that "the window goes blonde slowly" or Dylan Thomas's resolution to "enter again the round/Zion of the watery bead/And the synagogue of the ear of corn," he would have said that neither statement can be fitted into an ordered system of logical propositions, since neither statement exhibits a univocal relation between itself and an observable fact. Yes, both poetry and religion (or what Mr. Richards called the Magical View), since they rest upon "pseudo-statements," are utterly non-sensical, and it is foolish to debate the truthfulness of their assertions, truthfulness being a property only of referential or "certified scientific statements." But poetry has, at least, a medicinal value: it organizes and releases our impulses; and the poet therefore, in his role as physician, is to be tolerated.

The entire body of doctrine which Mr. Richards so zealously advocated in his early books is, I believe, quite thoroughly riddled with error and wrongheadedness, but it continues to be a focal point in this area of contemporary discussion, because it so well exhibits two characteristic tendencies of the modern secular mind: the first is its unwillingness to grant any cognitive power to the mythical and analogical language of poetry and religion; the second is its rather desperate desire, nevertheless, somehow to validate the life of the imagination, at least in its aesthetic phase, and its habit, therefore, of so increasing the superego of imaginative literature, of so heaping upon it responsibility for our salvation, as to make it in effect what Matthew Arnold made it—a surrogate for religion.

Now to this whole climate of opinion in our time certain representatives of religion and of poetry have reacted with extreme, and understandable, exasperation. On the one hand, there have been many who have despaired of setting up any significant conversation between the representatives of religion and the representatives of modernity, and who, being influenced by some of the more radical tendencies toward cultural separatism in recent theology (of the sort represented, say, by the thought of Dr. Karl Barth), have gone on not only to accept the sharp disjunctions between "reason" and "faith" of the positivists but to insist upon them, defiantly espousing in their own right the values of "faith." And, on the other hand, there have been many representatives of imaginative literature who, in reacting against the kind of salvationist program for the arts proposed by such spokesmen for the modern temper as Mr. I. A. Richards, have gone on to insist upon such an autonomy for poetry and the other verbal arts as would divorce them from all the other major areas of our value experience. The truth of Christ, for Dr. Barth, is something *totaliter aliter* than culture, and "God," he says, "is pure negation." While, on the other hand, Mr. W. H. Auden tells us that poetry is "not life and cannot be/A midwife to society," that it is "a game," and that

> What they should do, or how or when
> Life-order comes to living men
> It cannot say. . . .

But neither of these extreme reactions has, I believe, sufficient relevance to the cultural predicaments of our time; and both, though based upon partial truths, tend to support real error, as they are voiced by their less moderate exponents.

Few, certainly, would deny that Dr. Barth and his school in Protestant theology have performed a service of inestimable value for modern Christianity in recalling it to a sense of its distinctness, to a sense of the abiding tensions between itself and the enterprises of human culture and thus of the impossibility of any permanent *modus vivendi* between them. But surely Dr. Barth's strident declaration that there is no point of contact at all, no *Anknüpfungspunkt,* between the Christian gospel and the orders of culture is a much too drastic simplification of the delicate complexity of the problem. And, however understandable a result of our modern secular climate his extreme exacerbation may be, it hardly seems calculated to furnish the basis for any fruitful *rapprochement* between the Christian community and the larger community of the modern world.

One also has sympathy for the counterpart, on the side of art, to the Barthian reaction, in theology, with respect to the whole modern climate of positivistic secularism—the reaction that has assumed the form of the various theories in modern criticism of the autonomy of the aesthetic experience and activity. Poetry, says Mr. Allen Tate in the Preface to his volume *On the Limits of Poetry,* "is neither religion nor social engineering." And this has been a main lesson of many of the great critics of our time—of men like T. S. Eliot and R. P. Blackmur, John Crowe Ransom and Cleanth Brooks, and many others. The language of poetry, they have said, is not the language of science or of history or of metaphysics or theology. By which they do not at all intend to say that literature is utterly divorced from all concern with existential issues, as some of their less cogent disciples have suggested in their defense of a kind of "pure" poetry that makes no clean statement about anything at all. Nor do they mean, when they argue that poetic language does not properly eventuate in statements that *compete* with those of science and philosophy, what the positivists mean—that poetry is merely emotive. They do not, of course, want to impose such burdens upon poetry as Matthew Arnold proposed or as Mr. Richards once expected it to assume, for they know that the function of poetry is neither religious nor medicinal and that it cannot "save us." They do not regard the poet as a rhetorician conveying truths found in processes external to those of poetry and dressing out "propositions which could be stated more directly and more economically in abstract propositions." [28] But they yet regard poetry as in some sense cognitive, though critics like Mr. Tate and Mr. Brooks never cease reminding us that the poet's "truth" is given through his metaphors, which are his essential instruments for saying whatever it is that he has to say. And surely the discipline of reading the really great poems in our language—whether the poems be the later books of Henry James or the "Byzantium" poems of William Butler Yeats—bears them out in their contention that the language of poetry is the language of metaphor, the language of wit and paradox and irony. Which is, of course, to say, as the theorists of "autonomy" argue, that the language of poetry is untranslatable, in the sense that it dramatizes attitudes and beliefs in terms that are not interchangeable with the language of other types of discourse. So "nonsymbolic surrogates" [29] are not to be found for the language of poetry which keeps to its own symbolic forms. "For precisely in that symbolic form," said Wilbur Marshall Urban in his fine book, *Language and Reality,*

. . . an aspect of reality is given which cannot be adequately expressed otherwise. It is not true that whatever is expressed symbolically can be better expressed literally. For there *is* no literal expression, but only another kind of symbol. It is not true that we should seek the blunt truth, for the so-called blunt truth has a way of becoming an untruth. [30]

And yet literature, though it has its own special mode of existence and its own unique procedures, does obviously deal with what we call human experience. In so doing, however, it does not, to be sure, in so far as it is true to its own nature, seek to give us some extrapoetic truth, what Professor Urban called "blunt truth." It seeks to come to terms with human situations, and in so doing it gives us its special kind of symbolic truth which is different from the special forms of symbolic truth that science and religion give us. Its symbolic structures cannot be generalized out into the special types of notation employed by other forms of discourse, for poetry is the handmaid neither of science nor of religion. But these structures, in the greatest poetry, when properly read, will be found to contain reports and prophecies—and reports which religion certainly should be prepared to include among its evidences. Indeed, Mr. Tate has declared, perhaps a bit extravagantly, that "the high forms of literature offer us the only complete . . . versions of our experience." [31]

It is, therefore, altogether appropriate that those who are today seeking to relate the Christian faith to contemporary culture should be reading the important imaginative literature of our period and thinking about its significance for religious thought. And we may hope that the new attentiveness in the religious community to the verbal arts augurs what will be an increasing concern with these issues. "Theological study and discussion," as Professor Amos Wilder has said,

> give good heed today to contemporary movements in philosophy and science. They likewise concern themselves with the social phenomena of the time. But any true understanding of the modern situation requires similar attention to the deeper cultural factors as they reveal themselves in the arts and in related symbolic expression. This is evidently not just a matter of studying the uses of the arts in the church: church music, church architecture, sacred poetry and hymnology, and religious drama. It is rather a matter of observing and interpreting the modern arts generally: poetry, fiction, drama, criticism, painting, music, etc., viewed as indices of the modern crisis and of the spiritual alternatives and trends of the time. [32]

In order for this task—which Professor Paul Tillich calls the "theonomous analysis of culture" [33]—properly to be carried out, however, it is necessary, first of all, that the theological critic not be in too much of a hurry to find documentation of the *Zeitgeist* in the work of literary art under examination. He must be strictly concerned with the work of art as such, since that is the only relevant concern; and he must remember that poetry "is neither religion nor social engineering." There is, of course, a point, as Urban said, at which poetry may be seen to be "covert metaphysics," [34] but the theological critic, in relating the truths given in poetry to those which are within the custodianship of theology, should take care not to make of poetry, as did Matthew Arnold, "a kind of ersatz religion." [35]

But, then, the enterprise of a theological criticism of literature cannot even get under way if the attempt is made to ground it upon such an intemperately arrogant view of the relation of Christianity to culture as that which informs the extremer versions of that neo-Reformation theology which today comes out of Basel. For the Christian critic must, perhaps above all, have the humility to recognize, again as Professor Wilder has said, that the most remarkable feature with regard to the situation of the Christian heritage today is that its custody has to a considerable degree passed over into the keeping of secularized groups and forces. The disarray of institutional religion and the isolation of its more conservative bodies from modern life have left the gospel if not homeless at least in a highly ambiguous position. This has involved the "world" in a peculiar responsibility for the faith and in a process of travail with the faith, in considerable measure apart from the guidance of the church. In secular movements of thought, but especially in the arts and in imaginative literature, the vicissitudes of this struggle are disclosed.[36]

In other words,

large strata and movements in the western world are outside the church. But the religious tradition operates in them still in an indirect and disguised way. The river has gone underground; it has not ceased to flow.[37]

And those modern writers who have continued the explorations, the advance, and the witness of the Christian tradition "at a distance from the main body" Professor Wilder calls "the outriders of the faith"[38] who, though they may at times verge upon heresy, may yet in those very moments recall to us the truth that "the blood of the heretics is often the seed of the church."[39]

II

The Modern Experiment in Criticism:
A Theological Appraisal

Ours is a time in which, both life and thought being up against tremendous odds, we are all likely, in some degree or other, to be "crisis"-hunters, finding evidences of our general brokenness here, there, and everywhere. And, in my method of getting under way an estimate of the modern experiment in criticism, I do not myself propose to be an exception to the obsession of our age with *Tendenz,* since I suspect that any such estimate, from whatever point of view it may be undertaken, must begin by observing that criticism too is today in something like a situation of crisis. The crisis that I have in mind is one that arises out of what is central and decisive in the doctrines of modern poetics, and it was given a kind of desperate announcement a few years ago when Mr. Allen Tate bluntly raised the question which it is a peculiarity of our generation to be anxious about—namely, "is literary criticism possible?" [1]

It would not, of course, at first appear that the man of letters in our time feels himself to be at such an extremity, for one of the patron saints of the modern movement has assured us that the contemporary critic is "among the most presentable instances of modern man" and that in depth and precision his work is "beyond all earlier criticism in our language." And on all sides today we are frequently given similar testimonies of how unparalleled in any previous age are the vigor and trenchancy of criticism in our own time. So, with a zeal that is itself certainly unparalleled in any previous time, the contemporary movement is anthologized almost annually; and the editors of the journals in which it has gained expression frequently engage their colleagues in symposia the aim of which is to indicate the gains that have been made and the solid ground on which we may now take our stand. But in all this stocktaking I think we may sense a certain anxious uncertainty as to whether anything has been achieved at all and as to whether, in the presence of the great works of the past and of the modern period, we are yet able really to penetrate the ontological intransigence of the aesthetic fact. And it is just possible that, despite the actual impressiveness of the achievement of modern criticism, this anxiety is a consequence of the doctrine which it has promoted and which has had the ironical effect of calling into question the very possibility of criticism itself. Indeed, what I want to propose is that, if we will reconsider the basic premises of modern poetics, we may be put in mind not only of what in part our present distresses in criticism derive from but also of the special kind of testimony about contemporary criticism that it may be necessary for a theorist to make whose fundamental bearings are of a theological sort.

When we seek for the principal motives that underlie the general movement of criticism in our period, we cannot, of course, for long escape the recognition that, among them at least, has been the intention of many of its most distinguished representatives to offer some resistance to the reductionist tendency of modern scientism, particularly when it broaches upon those transactions with reality that are peculiar to the humanistic imagination. I can think of no single doctrine or emphasis that is subscribed to by all those writers who at one time or another have been held accountable for "the new criticism," but certainly by far a greater number of them are of a single mind in their apprehensiveness about the deeper cultural implications of the reigning positivism than they are on any other single point. And it has been their unwillingness to give their suffrage to the absolute hegemony of empirical science which has been a decisive influence upon their approach to the fundamental issues in theory of literature. Ours has been a time in which it has been generally supposed that the only responsible versions of experience that can be had are those afforded us by the empirical sciences and in which, therefore, the common impulse has been to trivialize the arts by regarding them as merely a kind of harmless play which, at best, is to be tolerated for the sedative effect that it has upon the nervous system. But even this assignment hardly constitutes a satisfactory charter for the artist, since, in the ministry of health to the nervous system, he is not likely to compete successfully with our modern doctors of psychology. So, in the last analysis, our culture has been incapable of finding for the arts, and especially for literature, a valuable or an irreplaceable function. And the result has been that the major strategists of modern criticism have felt it incumbent upon themselves to revindicate the poetic enterprise by doing what the culture was unable to do—namely, by seeking to define that unique and indispensable role in the human economy that is played by imaginative literature and that can be pre-empted by nothing else.

This contemporary effort to specify the nature of the autonomy which a work of literary art possesses has involved a careful analysis of what is special in the linguistic strategies of the poet. And the aim has been to establish that poetry is poetry and not another thing, for it has been recognized that in a culture as dominated by scientific procedure as is our own the common tendency is to hold all forms of discourse accountable to those critical canons that are really appropriate only to scientific modes of discourse—which, of course, then makes it possible for nonscientific modes of statement to be quickly dismissed on one pretext or another. So the tack that the contemporary movement in criticism has taken has been one that involves the denial that the poet is any sort of expositor at all. He is, we have been told, not an expositor, not a Platonist, not an allegorist, not a merchant in the business of ideas; on the contrary, he is a certain kind of technician, a certain kind of maker, who constructs out of language special sorts of things, such things as we call dramas and novels and poems. As the doctrine runs, what is distinctive about the language of imaginative literature is that, in contrast to the ordinary forms of discourse, it does not involve the reduction of words to the level of being merely conceptual signs. The mind is not led to appropriate the meaning of the individual components of a literary discourse by way of seeking those referents that are extrinsic to the discourse and to which its component terms presumably point. And our immunity from any compulsion to relate the language of the poem to an external reality has, in recent criticism, been understood in terms of the organic character of poetic structure. Which is to say that the contemporary critic has come to see poetic meaning not as a function of the relationships between the terms of the poem and some reality which is extrinsic to them, but rather as a function of the interrelationships that knit the terms together into the total pattern that forms the unity of the work. Our way of stating this distinctive character of poetic language is to say that its terms function not ostensively but reflexively, not semantically but syntactically—

by which we mean that, unlike the situation that obtains in logical discourse in which the terms "retain their distinctive characters despite the relationship into which they have been brought,"[2] in poetic discourse they lose their distinctive characters, as they fuse into one another and are modified by what Mr. Cleanth Brooks calls "the pressure of the context."[3] It is, indeed, this whole phenomenon to which Mr. Brooks has appropriately applied the term *irony,* a concept that he has insisted upon by way of emphatically remarking the radical extent to which the terms and "statements" of a literary work bear the pressure of the total context and have their meanings modified by that context. And it will be remembered that in a brilliant passage in *The Well Wrought Urn* he suggests that they ought even to be read as if they were speeches in a drama, since, as he says, if they are to be justified at all, it will not be by virtue of their "scientific or historical or philosophical truth, but [they will, rather, be] justified in terms of a principle analogous to that of dramatic propriety."[4]

Now it is in terms of this organic character of poetic structure that our generation has come to understand the resistance of literary art to the discursive paraphrase. It does not yield a series of paraphrasable abstractions because no set of terms of which a poetic work is constituted refers to anything extrinsic to the work: they refer, rather, to the other terms to which they are related within the work. And thus the perception of the meaning of the work awaits not an act of comparison between the component terms and the external objects or events which they may be taken to symbolize, but, rather, an act of imaginative prehension that will focus upon "the entire pattern of internal reference . . . apprehended as a unity."[5] The coherence of a work of imaginative literature is to be sought, in other words, not in any set of logically manageable propositions into which it may be paraphrased but rather in the living pattern of interrelated themes and "resolved stresses"[6] that the work contains.

There is, however, one inescapable fact that such a formulation of poetic meaning may at first appear to neglect, and it is the incorrigibly referential thrust that words do have. They like to function ostensively; that is to say, they insist upon pointing to things: it makes no difference whether the things are actual or ideal; what counts is that they are extrinsic to the words themselves, for the words are not happy unless they are performing a semantic function. And, this being their habit, it would seem that they would be intractable before the poetic purpose. But this problem is recognized by contemporary theorists who, indeed, have come to regard the poetic labor as involving in part an effort to deliver the word from its ordinary logical bonds and its inherent mediateness. As Mr. Ezra Pound once remarked, the poet "takes words ordinarily having conventional objective meanings, and by forcing them into a new and independent structure objectifies fresh meanings. . . . The function of the artist," said Mr. Pound, "is precisely the formulation of what has not found its way into language, i.e. any language, verbal, plastic or musical." [7] And it is precisely this effort of the poet to perform not simply an act of denotation but the far more difficult act of evocation, of capturing and conveying the full, living body of the world and of objectifying fresh experience of it—it is precisely this effort that very often commits him to the daring project of liberating words from the logical form into which they conventionally fall, so that they may be free to enter into the characteristic structures of poetic form in which they are affected by, and in turn affect, the total context established by the work. This is why you do not discover the meaning of a poem by taking an inventory of the various terms of which it is constituted and then by adding up the various meanings which these terms have in conventional usage. And when contemporary criticism insists upon the foolishness of such a procedure, it does so because it is sensitive, perhaps above all else, to the marvelous violence of the action that is performed upon terms once they are drawn up into the poetic process, so that each alters under the aspect of the other and enters relationships that are completely irreducible to logical form. It is the mystery that Mr. T. S. Eliot had in mind when he remarked upon "that perpetual slight alteration of language, words perpetually juxtaposed in new and sudden combination," which takes place in poetry.

So we may say, then, by way of summary, that the redefinition in our time of the nature of literary art has led to the view that the given work exists in and through its language. What we have immediately before us is a patterned mosaic in language which is, in the phrase by which M. Denis de Rougemont speaks of the work of art in general, "a calculated trap for meditation" [8]—and as such it effectively insists that before it we perform an act of rapt and "intransitive attention." [9] One might even say that for the modern sensibility the poetry in the poem resides "not [in] some intrinsic quality (beauty or truth) of the materials" [10] with which the poet builds his poem, but rather in the completeness of the unity or "composition" that he contrives out of the stuff of language. What we begin with, as Mr. Eliot has told us, is simply "excellent words in excellent arrangement." [11]

Now this redefinition in modern criticism of "the mode of existence of a literary work of art" has in turn led to a redefinition of the creative process. For so rigorous has been the stress that has been put upon the autonomy of poetic language till language itself has often very nearly been regarded as the enabling cause of literary art. It is assumed that art is a virtue of the practical intellect and that the poet's vision is not fully formed until it has become objectified in language. Indeed, the executive principle of the creative process is considered really to derive not from the poet's metaphysic or his special perspective upon the human story but rather from the medium to which his vision is submitted and by which it is controlled. It is regarded as a truism that whatever it is that the poet "says" about reality in a given work is something the content of which he himself did not fully possess until the completion of the work. For, as Mr. Murray Krieger has recently put it, "the poet's original idea for his work, no matter how clearly thought out and complete he thinks it is, undergoes such radical transformations as language goes creatively to work upon it that the finished poem, in its full internal relations, is far removed from what the author thought he had when he began." [12] The medium alone, in other words, objectifies the poet's materials and gives them their implications. This axiom of the contemporary movement in criticism is expressed with especial directness by Mr. R. P. Blackmur, when he remarks in his essay on Melville:

Words, and their intimate arrangements, must be the ultimate as well as the immediate source of every effect in the written or spoken arts. Words bring meaning to birth and themselves contained the meaning as an imminent possibility before the pangs of junction. To the individual artist the use of words is an adventure in discovery; the imagination is heuristic among the words it manipulates. The reality you labour desperately or luckily to put into your words . . . you will actually have found there, deeply ready and innately formed to give an objective being and specific idiom to what you knew and did not know that you knew.[13]

Whatever it is, in other words, that is in the completed work is there by virtue of the language which controls the creative process and which produces the "new word" that Mr. Yvor Winters declares the authentic work of literary art to be. The poet does not have a version of the human situation to express, some imperious preoccupation to voice, or some difficult report to make; no, he has none of this: indeed, as Mr. Eliot tells us, there is no good reason for supposing that he does "any thinking on his own" at all, for it is not his business to think—not even poets as great as Dante and Shakespeare. No, all the writer need have is his medium, and, if he knows how to trust it and how to submit to it, it will do his work for him: it will, as Mr. Blackmur says, bring the "meaning to birth."

Now, to be sure, what I have offered thus far is patently an abridgment of the advanced poetics of our time, but perhaps this account is at least sufficiently complex to provide some indication of the sources of the crisis that I earlier remarked as having arisen in contemporary criticism. It is clear certainly that we are being asked by many of the most distinguished theorists of our day to regard the work of literary art as a linguistic artifact that exists in complete detachment from any other independently existent reality. The fully achieved work of art, as the argument runs, is a discrete and closed system of mutually inter-related terms: the organic character of the structure prevents the constituent terms from being atomistically wrenched out of their context and made to perform a simple referential function, and it also succeeds in so segregating the total structure from the circumambient world as to prevent its entering into any extramural affiliation. "A poem should not mean but be," says Mr. MacLeish, and thereby, in this famous line from his poem "Ars Poetica," he summarizes, with a beautiful concision, the mind of a generation.

But, then, if the work of literary art exists in complete isolation from all those contexts that lie beyond the one established by the work itself, if it neither points outward toward the world nor inward toward the poet's subjectivity, if it is wholly self-contained and cut off from the general world of meaning, why then it would seem that nothing really can be said about it at all. And in this unpromising strait are we not all chargeable with "the heresy of paraphrase"? Mr. Mark Van Doren suggests in his book *The Noble Voice* that "Any great poet is in a sense beyond criticism for the simple reason that he has written a successful story," that "Criticism is most at home with failure," and that in the presence of the great success it must be "as dumb as the least instructed reader." [14] This is hardly an inspiriting conclusion for the practicing critic to reach; yet it is, in a way, the conclusion that has been enforced upon him by the new poetics of our period. For the curious irony that has arisen out of the contemporary movement in criticism is a result of the fact that, on the one hand, it has striven for a concept of literary art that would permit responsible discussion of it as art rather than as something else; but, on the other hand, it has succeeded in so completely segregating art from everything else till, in its presence, it has condemned itself, at least in principle, to silence. And this is, I believe, the reason for the noticeable anxiety in the critical forums today about whether anything has really been achieved at all. Much has been achieved, of course, in the establishment of a fund of substantiated judgments about literary texts, but the point is that this achievement has had no sanction in the body of principle to which our generation has come to subscribe, for that body of doctrine has tended ultimately to represent the aesthetic fact as unavailable for critical discussion. And thus it should perhaps, after all, not be surprising that the same distinguished critic who some years ago told us that the contemporary achievement surpassed "all earlier criticism in our language" is, in a more recent essay, to be found wondering why it is that critics don't go mad; and one of his equally distinguished friends often ruminates upon the "burden" that he and his colleagues in criticism today must bear.

The distresses and distempers that lead our most sensitive practical critics today to reflect upon the inhumanly difficult nature of their labors are, in other words, a result of their betrayal by the inadequate concept of literature that has descended to them from the main strategists in modern theory. There are many points at which this concept might now be put under some pressure, but that upon which I want to focus on this present occasion is the understanding of the creative process that has been promoted in our time, for here, I think, we may get as good a purchase as any other upon our present dilemmas. And when this aspect of modern theory is examined, it becomes evident to how great a degree its legislation about the nature of the poetic object has determined its understanding of the process by which that object is made. What it has wanted to insist upon is the indissoluble unity of form and content in the work which gives it the kind of autonomy that prevents its being translated into any other mode of statement. And this concern has in turn led contemporary theorists to minimize the controlling effect upon the creative process of the writer's ideas and beliefs. For it has been supposed that were any great tribute to be paid to these factors we should be quickly on the way toward reinstating the heresy of didacticism, with its notion that the literary work is merely a rhetorical communication of independently formulable ideas. So great stress has been put upon the directive role of the medium in the creative process, and we have been reminded of how radical must be the transformations of the poet's ideas, once these ideas undergo the modifications necessitated by the exigencies of a developing linguistic structure. What we are asked to understand is that nothing really exists in imaginative literature, except as it is organized by the medium which is language. Indeed, whatever does exist is itself created by the language, for, as Mr. I. A. Richards says, it is the "means of that growth which is the mind's endless endeavour to order itself" [15] —or, as Mr. Blackmur puts it in the passage which was quoted earlier, "Words bring meaning to birth and themselves contained the meaning as an imminent possibility before the pangs of junction." The medium, in other words, is a kind of intelligent agency which in some mysterious way puppetizes the poet and does the job for which, in its innocence, common sense has traditionally held him responsible.

I am aware that at this point I am to some extent exaggerating the contemporary testimony, but its own exaggerations in this matter are, I think, sufficiently great to make my characterization intelligible. In any event I am reassured by the coincidence that I discover between my own reaction and that of the English critic Mr. D. S. Savage, who suggests in the Preface to his book *The Withered Branch* that this "dizzy elevation" of the medium in contemporary criticism clearly leaves something important out of account.[16] And there is, I believe, no finer recent statement of what is unaccounted for than that which M. Jacques Maritain gives us in his great book *Creative Intuition in Art and Poetry*.[17]

In this book, which grew out of his Mellon Lectures that were given during 1952 in the National Gallery in Washington, M. Maritain brings to a point of culmination nearly forty years of study in the arts and in aesthetics. And in one of its aspects the book has it as a major concern to call into question the modern notion that the creative process in art is merely an *operational* process and that the artist is merely a special sort of technician. "As to the great artists," he says, "who take pleasure in describing themselves as mere engineers in the manufacturing of an artifact of words or sounds, as Paul Valéry did, and as Stravinsky does, I think that they purposely do not tell the truth, at least completely. In reality the spiritual content of a creative intuition, with the poetic or melodic sense it conveys, animates their artifact, despite their grudge against inspiration." [18] And this must be so, because, as M. Maritain insists, the activity which produces poetic art does not begin until the poet permits himself to be invaded by the reality of "Things" and until he himself seeks to invade the deepest recesses of his own subjectivity —the two movements of the spirit being performed together, as though one, "in a moment of affective union." When the soul thus comes into profound spiritual contact with itself and when it also enters into the silent and mysterious depths of Being, it is brought back to "the single root" of its powers, "where the entire subjectivity is, as it were, gathered in a state of expectation and virtual creativity." [19] And the whole experience becomes "a state of obscure . . . and sapid knowing." [20] Then

after the silent gathering a breath arises, coming not from the outside, but from the center of the soul—sometimes a breath which is almost imperceptible, but compelling and powerful, through which everything is given in easiness and happy expansion; sometimes a gale bursting all of a sudden, through which everything is given in violence and rapture; sometimes the gift of the beginning of a song; sometimes an outburst of unstoppable words.[21]

And only when this point in the artistic process has been reached may *operation* begin. For the artist to initiate the processes of *operation* at any earlier point is for him "to put the instrumental and secondary before the principal and primary, and to search for an escape through the discovery of a new external approach and new technical revolutions, instead of passing first through the creative source . . ." [22] Then what is produced is but "a corpse of a work of art—a product of academicism." [23] "If creative intuition is lacking," he says, "a work can be perfectly made, and it is nothing; the artist has nothing to say. If creative intuition is present, and passes, to some extent, into the work, the work exists and speaks to us, even if it is imperfectly made and proceeds from a man who has the habit of art and a hand which shakes." [24]

At "the single root" of the poetic process, then, there is a profound act of creative intuition. And in this cognitive act, says M. Maritain, the soul "suffers things more than it learns them," experiencing them "through resonance in subjectivity." The thing that is cognitively grasped is simply "some complex of concrete and individual reality, seized in the violence of its sudden self-assertion and in the total unicity" [25] that is constituted by "all the other realities which echo in this existent, and which it conveys in the manner of a sign." [26] And it is the richness of this imaginative prehension that gives life and power to the mathematic of poetic form.

M. Maritain is a good Thomist, and he does not therefore need to be reminded that art is "a virtue of the practical intellect" and that it requires "all the logic and shrewdness, self-restraint and self-possession of working intelligence." [27] Indeed, he insists upon the essential relation between art and reason, since it is reason that discovers the necessities in the nature of the medium that must be observed in order for the work to be brought into existence. But he also insists that the reason and the calculation that are in the poet "are there only to handle fire," [28] and that to grant them anything more than this purely instrumental function, simply for the sake of adherence to a puritanical formalism and a spurious austerity, is to be guilty of a gratuitous dogmatism.

Now many of us will doubtless find it difficult to accept M. Maritain's argument in this book in its entirety, for there are phases of his psychology—particularly those that bear upon his doctrine of the spiritual preconscious—that will surely strike us as exceedingly cumbersome and perhaps even slightly obscurantist. And I have adduced his testimony here not because it perfectly answers all of the questions that he raises. But, at a time when it is too much our habit to regard the medium as the single factor controlling the poetic process, M. Maritain's formulation of the problem has the very great merit of eloquently reminding us again of the actual primacy in the process of *poetic vision*. He discloses to us, that is, a stratagem for declaring once again that it is not language which brings "meaning to birth" and which enables the mind "to order itself"—not language, but *vision*.

Mr. Eliseo Vivas also helps us to some extent, I believe, with our difficulties when he reminds us that what is in part distinctive about the artist is his "passion for order." [29] "Really, universally," said Henry James, "relations stop nowhere, and the exquisite problem of the artist is eternally but to draw, by a geometry of his own, the circle within which they shall happily *appear* to do so." [30] That is to say, the artist wants to give a shape and a significance to what Mr. Vivas calls "the primary data of experience." He wants to contain the rich plenitude of experience within a pattern that will illumine and give meaning to its multifarious detail and its bewildering contingency. But, of course, he cannot discover such a pattern unless he has a vantage point from which to view experience and by means of which his insights may be given order and proportion. Which is to say that he can transmute the viscous stuff of existential reality into the order of significant form only in accordance with what are his most fundamental beliefs about what is radically significant in life, and these beliefs he will have arrived at as a result of all the dealings that he has had with the religious and philosophical and moral and social issues that the adventure of living has brought his way. The imaginative writer's beliefs, to be sure, are very rarely highly propositional in character: they do not generally involve a highly schematized set of ideas or a fully integrated philosophic system. He customarily has something much less abstract—namely, a number of sharp and deeply felt insights into the meaning of the human story that control all his transactions with the world that lies before him. And it is by means of these insights that he discovers "the figure in the carpet."

Mr. Graham Greene, in his criticism, has often liked to observe that "Every creative writer worth our consideration, every writer who can be called in the wide eighteenth-century use of the term a poet, is a victim: a man given to an obsession," [31] or to what he sometimes calls a "ruling passion." And I take it that when he speaks in this way he has in mind the poet's habit of loyalty to some discovered method of construing experience, to some way of seeing things, by means of which he grapples and comes to terms with the tumultuous and fragmentary world that presses in upon him. That is to say, I assume that Mr. Greene has in mind the act of consent which the poet gives to some fundamental hypothesis about the nature of existence which itself in turn introduces structure and coherence for him into the formless stuff of life itself. And it is indeed, I believe, this act that constitutes the real beginning of the poetic process: the rest is simply a matter of the kind of knowledgeable experimentation within the limits of his medium that the expert craftsman engages in till he discovers what he wants to say gaining incarnation within a given form.

Now I am aware that I must appear to be advocating a view of the poetic process which, in point of fact, I do not hold at all. For in much that I have just now said it may seem that I have been implying that, before even initiating the purely literary task, it is necessary for the poet to do an enormous amount of thinking. I have attributed to the writer's metaphysic or his beliefs a decisive role in the creative process, and thus it would seem I believe it necessary for the writer to engage in a great deal of abstract thinking before that process can even be initiated. But this I do not think is true at all. I do not, of course, want to associate myself with that tendency in modern literary theory which supports the supposition that the writer is not a thinker at all. This is a notion which Mr. T. S. Eliot has, I suppose, done more than anyone else to foster, and it is simply another instance of the confusion which his criticism, great as it is, occasionally contains. In his famous essay on "Shakespeare and the Stoicism of Seneca" he tells us, for example, that the poet does not "think" but that he makes poetry out of thought and that, therefore, he cannot *as poet* be said to "believe" in the system of thought that lies behind his poetry. In the particular case with which he is dealing, he tells us that Shakespeare did not really "think"; that he simply took the muddled and incompatible ideas of Seneca and Machiavelli and Montaigne and made poetry out of them. And Mr. Eliot having—and properly so—the enormous prestige in our time that he has, it is not surprising that our generation should have become for a time so convinced that Shakespeare was not a profound thinker, if he was a thinker at all; that he merely assimilated and felicitously re-expressed well-worn truisms. Or, again, in the case of Dante, he tells us that Dante did not "think" either; that he simply took the magnificent formulations of St. Thomas and used them as the foundation of his poem. But surely there is a great confusion here, for, as Fr. Martin Jarrett-Kerr has remarked, "If . . . we start from the initial conviction that one of the first marks of the major poet or novelist is the possession of a *fine mind,* we must refuse to concede that Shakespeare or Dante did not think but had their thinking done for them." [32]

Mr. Eliot's error here results, I suspect, from the supposition that to acknowledge the poet as a thinker is in effect to say that the poetic process originates in a highly developed *system* of ideas, and this is, of course, not at all the case. What I have been calling the writer's beliefs are rarely if ever the highly propositional things that Mr. Eliot, in denying them the importance which I have given them, seems to think they are. For what the writer generally has is not a *system* of belief but rather *an imagination* of what is radically significant.

So, in insisting upon the writer's necessary dependence upon his beliefs, I am not at all intending to suggest that the poet or the novelist must, first of all, be a philosopher or a theologian—though, on the other hand, I am not at all in accord with Mr. Eliot's contention that the poet is not really a thinker at all, a contention which is, by the way, significantly contradicted by Mr. Eliot's own career in poetry. There is a distinction somewhere in St. Thomas which illuminates, I think, the nature of the poet's relation to his beliefs. St. Thomas distinguishes between *cognitio per modum cognitionis*—knowledge, that is, in the manner of or by means of the intelligence or the discursive reason—and *cognitio per modum inclinationis,* knowledge, that is, in the manner of or by means of inclination. And what I would suggest is that the poet holds his "first principles" or his beliefs or his metaphysic *per modum inclinationis*—that is, inclinatorily. Which is to say that his beliefs point in the direction of a coherent philosophy of life toward which his sensibility has an irresistible inclination and in which it finds its necessary sanction. The contrast between the two modes of cognition is, to be sure, not an absolute contrast, and what it is therefore proper to say is that it is the *tendency* of the poet to hold his beliefs *per modum inclinationis,* though there are some writers, Mr. Eliot among them, who also hold their beliefs *per modum cognitionis.* But in whatever manner they may be held in the individual case, what I am now insisting upon principally is the precedence and the primacy of the act by which the poet searches experience and finds therein an ultimate concern that gives him then a perspective upon the flux and the flow.

Now whatever it is that concerns the poet ultimately, that constitutes his "ruling passion" and the substance of his *vision,* is something to which the critic can be attentive only as it is discoverable in the work. By now surely we have all taken to heart the lesson of Messrs. Wimsatt and Beardsley on "The Intentional Fallacy," and we understand the irrelevance of any essay in literary criticism that is based upon some process of armchair psychoanalysis which seeks to elevate the biographical category of the artist's conscious intention into a category of aesthetic discrimination.[33] But the designation of "intentionalism" as fallacious becomes itself a fallacy if it is made to support the view that a work of literary art is "a merely formal structure devoid of embodied meanings and values." [34] For such aesthetic objects, though "they may be found in the realm of pure design or pure music," [35] simply do not exist in the realm of literature where surely a main part of the critic's task involves the discovery of "the actual operative intention which, as telic cause, accounts for the finished work" [36] and which can be defined only in terms of the vision of the world which it serves. The authentic work of literary art, says M. de Rougemont, is a trap for the attention, but he also says that it is an "oriented trap." It is a trap, in the sense that, having the kind of autonomy that modern criticism has claimed for it, it "has for its specific function . . . the magnetizing of the sensibility, the fascinating of the meditation"; [37] as Mr. Vivas would put it, it can command upon itself an act of "intransitive attention." But the trap is "oriented": it *focuses* the attention, that is, upon something which transcends the verbal structure itself, this simply being the circumambient world of human experience, in those of its aspects that have claimed the poet's concern. And thus it is that the autonomy of the work is no more an absolute thing than is the intransitivity of the reader's attention, for both are qualified by the implicative relations that branch out indefinitely from the aesthetic fact toward the world by which that fact is surrounded.

Here it is, then, that we may discover the point of entry into the literary work that we have. For it is analysis of the sort that we have been conducting that reveals that the work is not a closed system and that it does not have that quality of "aseity" which Scholastic theologians have considered the Godhead to possess, by reason of the self-derived and eternally independent character of its being. The work is not wholly self-contained and utterly cut off from the reader, because, in the creative process, the aesthetic intentions of the artist are not segregated from all that most vitally concerns him as a human being but are, on the contrary, formed by these concerns and are thus empowered to orient the work toward the common human experience. This experience has, of course, to be grasped in and through the structures by means of which it is aesthetically rendered. But to stress the fact that poetic art signifies *by means of its structure* need not, I think, commit us to a formalism so purist as to require the view that the autonomy of the work is absolute. For, as I have been insisting, great literature does, in point of fact, always open outward toward the world, and that which keeps the universe of poetry from being hermetically sealed off from the universe of man is the poet's vision that it incarnates, of spaces and horizons, of cities and men, of time and eternity. This is why those modern theorists who tell us that the literary work is merely a verbal structure and that its analysis therefore involves merely a study of grammar and syntax—this is why they so completely miss the mark. They forget that writers use language with reference to what they know and feel and believe and that we can therefore understand their poems and novels only if we have some appreciation of how their beliefs have operated in enriching the meaning of the words that they employ. The poem-in-itself, in other words, as merely a structure of language, is simply a naked abstraction, for the real poem, the real novel, is something that we begin to appropriate only as we seek some knowledge of the context of belief and the quality of vision out of which it springs and with reference to which the words on the printed page have their fullest and richest meaning.

Now we have, I think, arrived at the point in our argument at which it is finally possible for me to turn to the generality of my subject, as it is formulated in the title of this chapter. For what I can now say is that the aspect of poetic art to which I have been referring by the terms *vision* and *belief* is precisely the element which we ought to regard as constituting the religious dimension of imaginative literature. When I speak of the religious dimension of literary art, in other words, I do not have in mind any special iconic materials stemming from a tradition of orthodoxy which may or may not appear in a given work. For were it to be so conceived, it might indeed then be something peripheral and inorganic to the nature of literature itself; whereas the way of regarding our problem that I now want to recommend is one that involves the proposal that the religious dimension is something intrinsic to and constitutive of the nature of literature as such. And I am here guided in my understanding of what is religious in the orders of cultural expression by the conception of the matter that has been so ably advanced by the distinguished Protestant theologian Paul Tillich. In all the work that he has done in the philosophy of culture over the past thirty years the persistent strain that is to be noted is one that arises out of his insistence upon what might be called the coinherence of religion and culture. He likes to say that "Religion is the substance of culture and culture the form of religion." [38] He has remarked, for example:

If any one, being impressed by the mosaics of Ravenna or the ceiling paintings of the Sistine Chapel, or by the portraits of the older Rembrandt, should be asked whether his experience was religious or cultural, he would find the answer difficult. Perhaps it would be correct to say that his experience was cultural as to form, and religious as to substance. It is cultural because it is not attached to a specific ritual-activity; and religious, because it evokes questioning as to the Absolute or the limits of human existence. This is equally true of painting, of music and poetry, of philosophy and science. . . . Wherever human existence in thought or action becomes a subject of doubts and questions, wherever unconditioned meaning becomes visible in works which only have conditioned meaning in themselves, there culture is religious.[39]

And Professor Tillich has acknowledged that it is to the theoretical comprehension of this "mutual immanence of religion and culture" that his philosophy of religion is primarily dedicated. "No cultural creation," he says, "can hide its religious ground," [40] and its religious ground is formed by the "ultimate concern" to which it bears witness; for that, he insists, is what religion is: it "is ultimate concern." [41] And since it is religion, in this sense, that is truly substantive in the various symbolic expressions of a culture, the task of criticism, in whatever medium it may be conducted, is, at bottom, that of deciphering the given work at hand in such a way as to reveal the ultimate concern which it implies. For, as he says, in the depth of every cultural creation "there is an ultimate . . . and [an] all-determining concern, something absolutely serious," [42] even if it is expressed in what are conventionally regarded as secular terms.

It should, of course, be said that, in these definitions, Professor Tillich is not seeking to *identify* religion and culture; but he does want to avoid the error that Mr. T. S. Eliot has cautioned us against "of regarding religion and culture as two separate things between which there is a *relation.*" [43] For what he recognizes is that the whole cultural process by which man expresses and realizes his rational humanity is actually governed by what are his most ultimate concerns—his concerns, that is, "with the meaning of life and with all the forces that threaten or support that meaning . . ." [44] And, in passing, it is, I think, worth remarking that it is this profoundly realistic approach to the problem of cultural interpretation that enables Professor Tillich to see that in our own period the most radically religious movements in literature and painting and music may gain expression in strangely uncanonical terms—in despairing maledictions and in apocalyptic visions of "the abyss" of disintegration that threatens the world today. For, as he would say, in the very profundity with which *Wozzeck* and the *Guernica* and *The Waste Land* express the disorder of the times there is an equally profound witness to the spiritual order that has been lost, so that these great expressions of the modern movement in art are rather like a confused and uncertain prayer that corresponds to the second petition of the *Our Father.* [45]

We are now, then, brought to the point at which we must regather our bearings by a final act of recapitulation. We have said that the work of literary art is a special sort of linguistic structure that traps the attention intransitively; but we have also argued that the intransitivity of the reader's attention is not absolute, since the autonomy of the object which captures his attention is not itself absolute. The literary work is a trap, but it is a trap that is *oriented* toward the world of existence that transcends the work—and the work is *oriented* by the *vision,* by the *belief,* by the *ultimate concern* of which it is an incarnation: its orientation, that is to say, is essentially religious. And this is why criticism itself must, in the end, be theological. The prevailing orthodoxy in contemporary criticism, to be sure, generally represents hostility toward the idea of metaphysical and theological considerations being introduced into the order of critical discourse. But, as Mr. Leslie Fiedler has remarked:

> The "pure" literary critic, who pretends, in the cant phrase, to stay "inside" a work all of whose metaphors and meanings are pressing outward, is only half-aware. And half-aware, he deceives; for he cannot help smuggling unexamined moral and metaphysical judgments into his "close analyses," any more than the "pure" literary historian can help bootlegging unconfessed aesthetic estimates into his chronicles. Literary criticism is always becoming "something else," for the simple reason that literature is always "something else." [46]

Our abdication from the reigning poetics of our time is, however, only partial, for the religious dimension of literature, as we have defined it, must be regarded as something which, in so far as it is really a datum for critical inspection and assessment, exists in the language of the work. For the only thing that lies before the critic is a composition in language, and it is, presumably, his skill in the supervision of language that primarily distinguishes the literary artist; surely it would be wrongheaded to assume that the thing that makes him an artist is the profundity or the novelty of his vision: no, he makes good his vocational claim in the republic of letters by the extent of the success with which he shapes the substance of experience, in accordance with his vision of what it is that makes it ultimately meaningful. And he can give a significant form or shape to experience only in so far as he takes the highest kind of advantage of the medium in which his art is wrought. So it may then, I think, be taken for granted that whatever it is that *orients* a work of literary art or that constitutes the *ultimate concern* that it embodies is something that will disclose itself in the ways in which the writer brings the resources of language into the service of his project. And thus we shall want very carefully to preserve all that has been gained in modern criticism as a result of its methodological researches into the problem of how the language of imaginative literature is to be understood and talked about. But for the critic to insist upon remaining merely a kind of grammarian is for him to forgo many of the most interesting and significant discriminations that literary criticism can make. For, though the literary work is a special sort of linguistic structure, that which holds the highest interest for us is the special seizure of reality which this structure is instrumental toward. It is, in other words, the nature of literature itself that compels the critic finally to move beyond the level of verbal analysis to the level of metaphysical and theological valuation. On this level, of course, he can establish the propriety of his judgments only by reference to his own insight, his own scale of values, his own sense of what is important in art and in life. And, as the English critic, the late S. L. Bethell, remarked:

. . . if he is a Christian worthy of the name, his whole outlook will be coloured by his religion; he will see life in Christian terms, and, though he may ignore an atheist writer's professed atheism, he will still judge his degree of insight into character by his own insight, which will have been formed in part by his Christian experience. And the non-Christian critic—let us be clear about this—will also judge a writer's insight into character (or into anything else, of course) by the standard of his own insight, however derived. There is no "impartial criticism" in this sense, or rather there is no critical neutrality; there are only Christian critics and Marxist critics and Moslem critics—and critics who think themselves disinterested but who are really swayed unconsciously by the beliefs they have necessarily acquired by being members of a particular society in a particular place and time.[47]

And, as Bethell observed with great shrewdness,

the last are really the least impartial, for, believing themselves impartial, they are open to every unconscious influence upon their judgment, while the "doctrinaire" critic may keep his doctrine well in view and, if not entirely avoiding prejudice, may at least give his readers fair warning of what to expect.[48]

But now at this point the question may well be raised as to whether my use of these quotations from Bethell is calculated to suggest that we are justified in trying to guarantee literary art by the quality of belief that it possesses. And, were this question to be put to me, my impulse, as a Christian, would, I think, be to say, with Professor Roy W. Battenhouse, that "the good poet should be able, like Adam in the Garden, to name every creature correctly. Apprehending the form of each thing that is brought before him, he should be able to assign it its proper place." [49] But, of course, this capacity, which so influentially determines the outcome of the artistic process, is itself very largely dependent upon the artist's metaphysical or religious orientation—so that, as a Christian, I should again feel prompted to say, with Mr. Battenhouse, that if it is true that the light with which an artist sees inclines to affect the justness of his observations, the presence of full light cannot but clarify the issues of proportion and order. With inadequate lighting, the artist will not see certain things he ought to see; it will be all too easy for him to draw disproportionately what he does see. To put it another way the artist who takes up his location in Plato's cave has not the same chance as he who sets up shop by Christ's open tomb.[50]

In principle, I should, in other words, expect the Christian reader at least—all other things being equal—more enthusiastically to give his suffrage to a literature that was Christianly *oriented* than to one which was not. But now, not as a matter of principle but as a matter of fact, the Christian reader lives in a period whose characteristic quality, at least ever since the Renaissance, has been defined, as Mr. Erich Heller has reminded us, not merely by a dissociation of faith from knowledge but by what has been the profounder severance of faith from sensibility. "It is this rift," says Mr. Heller, "which has made it impossible for most Christians not to *feel,* or at least not to feel *also* as true many 'truths' which are incompatible with the truth of their faith." [51] They have, in other words, been in very much the same position that the father of the possessed child was in whom the Synoptist records as having cried out: "Lord, I believe; help thou mine unbelief" (Mark 9:24). And, this being the case, the Christian reader will actually respond to the various constructions of the human story that he encounters in literature with a latitudinarianism that will, at least in part, be akin to that which any other sensitive reader in our time brings to bear upon his dealings with literary art: that is to say, what he will require is that the view of life that is conveyed by the given poem or novel commend itself as a possible view, as one to which an intelligent and sensitive observer of the human scene might be led by a sober consideration of the facts of experience. And, though he will agree with Mr. Eliot that to judge a work of art by artistic standards and to judge it by religious standards ought perhaps to "come in the end to the same thing," [52] he will recognize, as Mr. Eliot does, that, in our time, this is an end at which most of us will have great difficulty in arriving.

But, hesitant as the Christian critic in our time ought to be in defining for himself a program whose rigor would have the effect of delimiting the range of his sympathies and of isolating him from the actualities of the literary life, we may yet, I think, put to him the question as to what in general will be his approach to the literature of our own period. Here we must remember, as Professor Amos Wilder has so well said, that "the most significant art of the twentieth century—Stravinski, Picasso, Joyce, Kafka, Pound, Eliot—is that which comes immediately out of the epochal convulsions of the time, out of full immersion in the condition of man today." [53] And, this being the case, we should not be surprised that "the fountains of spiritual renewal" in literature, as Professor Wilder says, have often broken forth "outside the churches in uncanonical witness, prayer and celebration." [54] The crypto-religious character of many of the basic impulses in modern literature has, of course, often been remarked upon, and we must remain mindful that the artist's failure to canalize these impulses in the direction of explicit Christian affirmation is, very frequently, not to be construed in terms of his own agnosticism and intransigence but, rather, in terms of the Christian community's failure to present itself to him as something with which he might really make common cause. This is why "the protagonists of traditional values, the witnesses of the older covenants and charters of our common life, the saints in the sense of the dedicated and disciplined individuals who assume the costs of nonconformity, the martyrs or scapegoats of the general crisis"—this is why all these are often "found in secular guise, unordained except by the authenticity of their utterance." [55] And the recognition of these ambivalences and dislocations by the Christian critic must be the starting point, I believe, of any transaction into which he may enter with the world of modern art.

The great effort of the Christian critic in our day should have as its ultimate aim a reconciliation between the modern arts and the Church, between the creative imagination and the Christian faith. The immense obstacles on the side of art and on the side of the Church that hinder this achievement are, however, not to be minimized. The great misfortune is that those modern writers who have experienced most profoundly the intellectual and spiritual predicaments of the time and whose return to Christianity would therefore be most arresting are often those who are most acutely sensible of the failure of institutional Christianity—and especially of Protestantism—to give due place to "the yea-saying impulse of the biblical faith and its moment of creative play." [56] It is felt "that a Christian so sterilizes his heart that there is no concern left for art and the rich play, the riot and fecundity of life." [57] It is the rejection of a Christianity (and generally a Protestant Christianity) that is felt to be ascetical and world-denying which forms the rule among modern writers rather than the exception: Yeats and

Joyce and Wallace Stevens and many others have refused the Gospel, very largely, one feels, because of the failure of its interpreters to express what Professor Wilder feels to be the genuine element of antinomianism in the Gospel itself.[58] He puts the issue with great clarity in his book *The Spiritual Aspects of the New Poetry:*

For the poets the scandal of Christ is his asceticism. The very medium of their art as poets; indeed, the very element of their experience as men, is the gamut of human living, emotions, drama. "Man's resinous heart" and the loves, loyalties, the pride, the grief it feeds—these are the stuff of poetry and the sense of life. And the Cross lays its shadow on this; it draws away all the blood from the glowing body of existence and leaves it mutilated and charred in the hope of some thin ethereal felicity. The wine of life is changed to water. . . . The "dramatic caves" of the human heart and imagination are renounced for some wan empyrean of spiritual revery. The very word "spiritual" has come to signify inanity and vacuity. The refusal of religion by the modern poet, and by more than moderns and by more than poets, goes back to the apparent denial of human living by religion, to the supposed incompatibility of life with Life and of art with faith.[59]

That this is the major hindrance on the side of art to a reconciliation between the creative imagination and the Church one may very quickly discover by a perusal of one of the most interesting spiritual documents of our period, the *Partisan Review* symposium, *Religion and the Intellectuals* (1950), in which the general testimony of many of the most influential literary figures of our day tends to confirm Professor Wilder's assessment.

There are also serious hindrances on the side of the Church to a *rapprochement* between art and faith. There are many religious people who suppose their own conservative and unaroused attitudes toward modern life to be based upon valid Christian principles, when they really derive from a protected social situation in which it has been possible for them to shut their eyes to the dislocations of the age to which history has committed both them and ourselves. They face with defensiveness and hostility much of modern literature in which these stresses and strains are reflected, and they insist upon the excessiveness of its alarmism and its irrelevance to the world in which they choose to believe that they live. It is their habit to speak of many of the major writers of this century—Pound and Gide, Joyce and Lawrence, Kafka and Faulkner—as if the difficulties presented by their work were merely frivolous and as if the inclination of their vision toward a tragic perspective were a consequence merely of their morbidity or even of

the disorder in their personal lives. And they mistake their censorious-
ness with respect to the modern artist for a genuinely Christian position. A more sophisticated version of the same unfriendliness to the
modern arts arises out of the extreme disjunctions between the natural
order and the order of revelation that are insisted upon in those currents of Protestant thought stemming from Crisis Theology. In this
theological framework the arts, as a department of human culture, are
comprehended in terms of their issuance from the natural order, all of
whose fruits are, of course, to be viewed, as a matter of principle, with
a deep suspicion and skepticism.

The difficulties, in other words, that hinder reconciliation in our day
between the modern artist and the Christian Church seem to be, as
Professor Wladimir Weidlé has suggested in his penetrating essay *The
Dilemma of the Arts,* difficulties of "mutual incomprehension." [60]

One thing, however, is, I believe, fairly certain, and that is that the
Christian community will not succeed in relating itself creatively to
the modern artist if it attempts to do so by laying down its law, by
hedging him about with rules and programs to be followed and carried
out. Its proper course is perhaps most clearly set forth in a set of distinctions that Professor Tillich has made central to his philosophy of
culture. Those who are familiar with his thought will recall that there
are three terms for which he has a great liking: he often speaks of
"autonomy," of "heteronomy," and of "theonomy," and it will at this
point be helpful for us to put ourselves in mind of what is at issue in
the distinctions that he draws between these terms. In each case, it will
be noticed, the suffix derives from the Greek *nomos,* meaning usage
or the law of human life; so the three terms stand for different versions
of what the nature of that law is.

The prefix of the first, autonomy, derives from the Greek *autos,*
meaning "self"; and thus the term points to that view of the law of life
which suggests that man is himself the source of it and that the culture
which he creates is not therefore to be measured by reference to any
ultimate principle transcendent to the rational and the human. The
prefix of the second term, heteronomy, derives from the Greek *heteros,*
meaning "that which is other than, different from, alien to, strange";
so, when Professor Tillich uses this term, he has in mind those ecclesi-
astical and political communities that relate themselves to the enterprises of culture by hedging them about with laws and authoritative
criteria that are not organic to their nature. Finally, the prefix of the
third term has its origin in the Greek word *theos,* meaning "god," and

Professor Tillich employs the concept of theonomy to designate that view of culture which understands the divine law to be "at the same time, the innermost law of man himself," [61] which regards the transcendent as being not a dimension external to, and therefore to be imposed upon, man's cultural life but rather as the inescapable spiritual ground of all our art and philosophy and science. Autonomy, in other words, represents the attempt to cut the ties of a culture with its transcendent ground, with anything ultimate and unconditional; heteronomy represents "the attempt of a religion to dominate autonomous cultural creativity from the outside," [62] while a theonomy is "a culture in which the ultimate meaning of existence shines through all finite forms of thought and action; the culture is transparent, and its creations are vessels of a spiritual content." [63]

Now Professor Tillich's excellent point is that the way of heteronomy can never be the way of Protestantism. A truly Protestant orientation to culture must, to be sure, also involve a criticism of "self-complacent autonomy," but always, he insists, the Protestant community, when it is true to its own informing principle, will remember that "in the depth of every autonomous culture an ultimate concern, something unconditional and holy, is implied." And the genius of Protestant Christianity is most truly expressed when, in its dealings with what is called "secular culture," it so takes this body of witness up into itself that the distinction between the sacred and the secular ceases to exist.

It will, I believe, be along this way—the way of "theonomy"—that a reunion of art and religion, if it is to occur at all, will be achieved. But, of course, what will be chiefly required is an infinite degree of tact and humility in the Christian critic, and thus a reconciliation between art and faith in our day would be, as Professor Weidlé has said,

the symptom of a renewal of the religious life itself. When frozen faith melts again, when it is once more love and freedom, then will be the time that art will light up again at the new kindling of the fire of the spirit. There seem to be many indications that such a future is possible; and in any case it is the only future still open to art. There is one way alone—and there is no other—because artistic experience is, deep down, a religious experience, because the world art lives in cannot be made habitable save by religion alone.[64]

Prolegomenon to a Christian Poetic

IN RECENT YEARS one of the most hopeful and promising events in our cultural life has been the new and fresh encounter between religion and imaginative literature. The steadily increasing closure of the hiatus that for so long existed between them has been the result of exploratory movements of the spirit on both sides of the boundary line over which they hover. The modern writer, on the one hand, in his reflection upon the issues of existence that in a time of crisis have engaged the modern imagination, has often found himself peering into those vacuums of tragedy and mystery whose terrors it has traditionally been the office of religion to assist us in confronting. And, on the other hand, the most sensitive interpreters of the Christian faith, in their efforts to speak to the disintegrated consciousness of modern man, are often turning today to this whole body of confessional literature in order to discover a point of entry into the country of the mind inhabited by the men of our time. Thus it is that, as one critic has said, the custodians of these two departments of our imaginative life are seeking once again to "Learn from each other where their love will/lead them."

This new meeting between the poetic and the theological mind has, of course, its dangers, the most serious of which perhaps is the likelihood that the functions of poetry may be confused with those of religious testimony or of the cultural documentation of the *Zeitgeist*. And, were this to happen, neither poetry nor religion would be well served by the confusion, for at so late a date as this any recapitulation of the errors of Matthew Arnold, or of the nineteenth century generally, can only involve an emasculation of religion and a further enfeeblement of poetry. This is not at all to say that blanket endorsement must be given to all the extremist doctrines of the autonomy of poetry which recent literary theory has put forward; but surely, in this connection as in all others, the health of the mind is not benefited by falsely identifying those things which are in fact discrete and different.

It appears, then, that for our time one of the most important enterprises of Christian thought to be engaged in is that which will seek to arrive at a distinctively theological understanding of the literary imagination, at once in its characteristic identity and in its relation to those procedures of the mind and the heart which constitute the religious mode of vision. We find ourselves at this point, however, before a body of questions on which the articulated traditions of Protestant thought —in contrast to those of the Church of Rome—have little light to throw. Indeed, an examination of the main lines of development in theory of literature from Lessing and Coleridge down to I. A. Richards and the early T. S. Eliot would hardly reveal to an inquiring visitor in the Western world, making his first acquaintance with the usages of our culture, that such a thing as Protestant Christianity had ever existed. So, as we try today to discover what might be the first principles of a Christian poetic, it must be realized that we are breaking fresh ground and that for a time we must inevitably be groping somewhat in the dark.

I should like at this juncture, however, to suggest that we may perhaps get our bearings in relation to this whole range of issues if we return to the point at which much of the most fruitful renewal of Christian thought in our time has been realized. And this is the point at which we have recovered in Protestant theology an understanding of the dynamics of the world of interpersonal relations. We have here, of course, been most greatly helped perhaps not by a Christian theologian principally but rather by the most remarkable Jewish philosopher of our time, Martin Buber, the themes of whose thought have impregnated recent Christian theology to an incalculable degree. The main contours of Dr. Buber's philosophy are to be traced in many of his writings, but the most concentrated expression of his ideas is still to be found in his little book *I and Thou,* which, in the years since its first appearance in 1923, has become well-nigh a modern classic. And here there is revealed, at the heart of his thought, a radical disjunction between what he considers to be the two most fundamental modes in which man may relate himself to the world. He may relate himself to things or objects or to what Dr. Buber calls the world of "It," which comprises all the things that we experience and use, all the things that we arrange and organize and manipulate; this is, primarily, the world

of science and technology. Or, Dr. Buber tells us, we may relate ourselves not to things but to other persons, in which case we enter the
world of "Thou," for here we no longer weigh and measure and judge
and control. No, here we are addressed, and we must respond; and
thus the individual is no longer the sole arbiter of the situation, since it
includes, besides himself, another independent center of intelligence
and volition—and between these two the relation is that of an *I* to a
Thou who is not to be experienced or used but who is to be *met* in
relation.

When life is lived in the dimension of the I-It relation, it is
governed by the compulsions of the private ego, and in this awful
solitariness all that a man knows is "the feverish world outside and
his feverish desire to use it. . . . He has in truth no destiny, but only
a being that is defined by things and instincts, which he fulfills with
the feeling of sovereignty—that is, in the arbitrariness of self-will." [1]
His world is cluttered up only with his private obsessions and his individual purposes, and this is why he is "emptied of reality." [2] Indeed,
the constitutive principle of his world is individuality—not relation,
but individuality, which Dr. Buber defines as the quality of "being
differentiated from other individualities." [3] "Individuality," he says,
"revels in its special being" and "neither shares in nor obtains any
reality. It differentiates itself from the other, and seeks through experiencing and using to appropriate as much of it as it can. This is *its*
dynamic, self-differentiation and appropriation, each exercised on the
It within the unreal." [4] It "is concerned with its My—my kind, my race,
my creation, my genius." [5] And, of course, the more the individual
encloses himself within the prison walls of his own ego, the less is his
relation with life and reality. "The more a man . . . is mastered by
individuality, the deeper does the *I* sink into unreality. In such times
the person in man and in humanity leads a hidden subterranean and
as it were cancelled existence—till it is recalled." [6]

But in the world of "Thou" life is lived in quite a different dimension: it is lived in love. And here, says Dr. Buber,

is the cradle of the Real Life, [for] love is *between I* and *Thou*. The man
who does not know this . . . does not know love. . . . In the eyes of him
who takes his stand in love, and gazes out of it, men are cut free from their
entanglement in bustling activity. Good people and evil, wise and foolish,
beautiful and ugly, become successively real to him; that is, set free they
step forth in their singleness, and confront him as *Thou*. . . . Love is responsibility of an *I* for a *Thou*. In this lies the likeness . . . of all who love,

from the smallest to the greatest and from the blessedly protected man, whose life is rounded in that of a loved being, to him who is all his life nailed to the cross of the world, and who ventures to bring himself to the dreadful point—to love *all men*.[7]

And Buber's point is that it is only in this dramatic context of relationship, of meeting, that the individual becomes truly a person; he who does not enter into the relational event, who insists upon remaining within the alienation of the single, isolated self, does not become a man, does not enter into the fullest possession and enjoyment of his humanity. But "When *Thou* is spoken, the speaker . . . takes his stand in relation."[8] And in this world of *I* and *Thou,* man no longer goes out to exploit and use things; no, he goes out to meet and enter into vital relationship with others.

The meeting with the *Thou* has, however, not only a horizontal but also a vertical dimension, for, as Dr. Buber reminds us, through contact with every particular *Thou* we are "stirred with a breath" of the eternal *Thou,* in whom the extended lines of all relations meet. The choice, in other words, of mutuality, of relationship, of meeting, is the choice of eternal life: the choice of relationship with other beings is the choice of relationship with Being itself.

Now it should be noted at this point that, though Dr. Buber regards the personal relation, at its best, as affording us the clearest glimpse of and the surest transport to the ultimate Ground of Being, he would readily admit that the "I-Thou" relation need not be regarded as a possibility only for the relation between persons. Indeed, his conviction seems rather to be that it is the thing to be striven for at every point in our dealings with the universe, for every nonhuman creature and every natural occurrence or object, he would say, has the power of "speaking" to us, of penetrating that restless, diurnal world of familiarity in which we normally live, and of stirring the soul to new apprehension and response. And he would agree with Professor Philip Wheelwright, who says at one point in his book, *The Burning Fountain:* "To regard anything honestly as a *thou* means, first, to value it intensely for its own sake, and secondly, to accept a potential interchange of roles with it—to let it speak as an *I* while I myself become a listener."[9] And for the self so to confront its object—whether it be a dog or a tree or some vast and awesome projection of the earth's terrain—is for it to become itself, in these strangely lyrical and dramatic moments, a *thou* before the presence of that object.

The world of "It" is, then, not at all impermeable by the gracious spirit that pervades the world of "Thou"; on the contrary, a main part of our human task is to try to see to it that the walls of separation that divide these two worlds from each other are broken down, so that the whole of life may be gloriously resurrected into the radiant fullness of *Thou*hood.

Now, to be sure, Dr. Buber's philosophy does not rest explicitly upon a theology of the Incarnation; and yet, in one beautifully lambent sentence that seems in a way to sum up his whole vision of things, when he says, "All real life is meeting," we feel that here is an understanding of life that is proximately Christian. For surely much (though by no means all) of what the Christian faith has to say about reality consists essentially in the declaration that we live in a "spiritually responsive" universe which, in all its myriad reaches, invites us to enter into an I-Thou relationship with it.[10] And this is the assertion that is at the center of Dr. Buber's entire philosophy.

But if we are to become fully aware of the relevance of this view of life to the whole of human thought and culture, we must recognize that it implies not only a metaphysical and an ethical principle but also an aesthetic principle, a canon of judgment and criticism relevant to the entire range of issues of discrimination in literature and the arts. For to seek in all our relations with the world about us to achieve the I-Thou relation is no longer to regard the world, in any of its aspects, as destined for our use or exploitation: its objects, its creatures, are rather to be regarded as beings with whom one enters into living relationship. They are to be regarded not merely in terms of their practical significance, not merely in terms of their potential capacity to help or hinder us in the fulfillment of our daily practical purposes, but they are to be valued for their own dear sakes and for the diverse ways in which they glorify the Lord. The sixth-century monk Cassiodorus declared: "God is really wonderful and extremely wise in having distinguished every one of his creatures by a unique dispensation lest unseemly confusion overwhelm them."[11] And it has been too little noticed in the main traditions of Protestant theology that the attainment of a truly sacramental conception of life involves the undertaking of an essentially contemplative discipline or *askésis* whose purpose it will be to assist the mind in directly confronting the individual presences with which the world is filled. The fullest apprehension of the glory of the created world rests always, in other words, upon such a sensitive awareness of the particular and the unique in experience, in all their rich unicity, as will make it possible for us to enter into I-Thou relationships with them when we meet them. St. Teresa tells us: "I require of you only to look"—and this, one feels, is an essentially Christian demand: *look* at

> sea monsters, and all deeps;
> Fire and hail, snow and vapor;
> Stormy wind. . . .
> Mountains and all hills;
> Fruitful trees and all cedars;
> Beasts and all cattle;
> Creeping things and flying birds;

and, above all, look at men, at

> Kings of the earth and all peoples;
> Princes and all judges of the earth;
> Both young men and virgins;
> Old men and children. . . .[12]

For, until you have looked at life and the creatures of the world, there is no possibility for you of meeting them in the relationship of *I* and *Thou*, of meeting them in love and in the spirit of praise.

So, when the Christian man is asked what it is that he demands of the artist or the poet, he must answer, it seems to me, that he demands of the poet what is demanded of himself but what the poet, by reason of his special gifts, is enabled to do with enormously greater intensity —namely, to look at and to contemplate the created world; and then, of course, he will say that it is the vocation of the poet so to incarnate his vision in poetic form as to trap the rest of us into a similar act of meditation. The poet, in other words, as Mr. Allen Tate has said in his remarkable essay on "The Symbolic Imagination," "has got to do his work with the body of this world, whatever that body may look like to him, in his time and place—the whirling atoms, the body of a beautiful woman, or a deformed body, or the body of Christ, or even the body of this death." [13] His vigilance is the vigilance of a man upon whom the natural order of common things is pressing all the time, and his great gift to the rest of us is a fuller disclosure of the order of the world in which we live. And when he knows his business and is strong, he does not collapse into eternities or abysses, into Platonic heavens or into Realms of Essence, until he has sailed throughout the vast sphere of our natural condition. His patron saint is not Dionysius the Areopagite but St. Athanasius, for, in his dealings with the body of this world, his Way is not the Way of Rejection but rather the Way of Affirmation.[14]

He seeks, in other words, to translate into the actualities of poetry not the light that never was on land or sea but, rather, the light of ordinary day. And it is precisely for this reason, it seems to me, that the Christian man must value so highly the contribution of the artist to human culture, for he traps us into what Professor H. A. Hodges has called "the disinterested stare of contemplation," [15] which, however strenuous an exercise it may be for us, is a necessary precondition for the achievement of the kind of "I-Thou" relationship with the things of this world for which the Christian imagination yearns.

This, then, I am suggesting, may be regarded as a properly Christian understanding of the office and work of the poet: his vocation—and really it is a human vocation of us all, in so far as our native endowment of sensibility enables us to accept its burden—is to *stare,* to *look* at the created world, and to lure the rest of us into a similar act of contemplation. And, of course, it is in the order of common things that "the great diagrams are perceived; from them the great myths open; by them," as the late Charles Williams said, we understand "the final end." [16]

But what we have now to remember is that the steadily intent contemplation of the created world, in all its tremendous variety and plenitude, is precisely the attitude of mind that has proved so difficult for the modern poet to achieve. For his ontological moorings have been broken, and his Way has not been the Way of Affirmation but the Way of Rejection, which, instead of leading further and further into the complexities of the natural order, has led deeper and deeper into the unpromising world of his own "voided interiority." [17] Nor does the genesis of this abdication lie in the immediate past; its location is rather to be found in that disastrous moment long ago when, as the late Archbishop Temple said, "René Descartes, having no claims to meet, remained for a whole day 'shut up alone in a stove.' " [18] For it was in that moment that many of the most perplexing dilemmas of modern culture were born, the moment in which Descartes, resolving to doubt all things, decided that there was one thing which could not be doubted—namely, his own existence as a thinking being. It may be that I take a highly jaundiced and melancholy view of this commanding genius of the seventeenth century, but, as Mr. Allen Tate has remarked, "The demonology which attributes to a few persons the calamities of mankind is perhaps a necessary convention of economy in discourse." [19] And as we try to understand the forces in the modern world that have been responsible for the flight of our poets and artists into the various forms of subjectivism to which they have been dedicated, we must recognize in Descartes a major strategist of our culture, for it is from him that several major tendencies in the history of the post-Renaissance mind derive.

The Cartesian *cogito* was only a starting point from which he proceeded to accept as true only those things which could be perceived clearly and distinctly. Following this tack, he arrived at the self-evident idea of God, and thence he arrived at the serene conviction that his perceptions of the physical world were not to be distrusted, since, to the God who was their primal cause, neither caprice nor malicious deceptiveness could be attributed. And all of this—his certainty of his own existence, of God's existence, and of the extended world's existence —was, he believed, a deduction from clear and simple ideas, from innate intuitions. Nor was he at all greatly troubled by the drastic rigor with which he had sundered the world of self-conscious thought and the world which is extended in space, for he was so bent upon affirming the complete autonomy of the human reason that he never deeply realized how completely he had severed the mind from reality and with what finality he had shut it in upon its own processes.

This was, indeed, the main bequest of the Cartesian spirit to the modern age, what Hegel called "the principle of interiority." And it might well be argued that Hamlet was, in a way, the first great hero of the new period (though Shakespeare came directly at his own philosophic skepticism by way of Descartes's predecessor, Montaigne), for here is the modern individual shut up within the awful prison of the mind, his "native hue of resolution . . . sicklied o'er with the pale cast of thought," his soul overborne by the enervating disease of solipsism.

Yet Spengler was surely right in regarding Goethe's Faust as presenting us with what is perhaps the largest image of the modern spirit, with *the* classic instance of the exacerbated modern sensibility. For here we have the modern rationalist intellectual, uncommitted to the living body of the physical world, who, after years of pursuing scientific studies, is finally overcome with a sense of utter failure, with a deeply enervating disillusionment and despair. He has sought to fathom the innermost secrets of the natural order, yet, amid the isolation of his scholar's chamber, he has lived in complete separation from all the living forms of nature. His residence has been in the Cartesian vacuum, where the thing to be pursued is the clear and distinct idea, the high abstraction—which is, of course, utterly incommensurable with the rich complexity of the concrete object in which reality has its actual incarnation. And this he begins to realize, as he cries out to Nature, "Oh, could I but cleanse away the soot of learning and wash myself sound in your dew!" and as he curses himself, on looking about at the four walls of his study, for being still "stuck in this prison. . . . This damned damp hole in the wall where the sweet light of heaven breaks gloomily through the painted panes!" "Instead of living nature in which God created man," he tells himself, "you're surrounded by smoke and rot, animals' skeletons and dead men's bones." But he has chosen a drought for which, as M. Jacques Maritain has said, "romantic tears . . . provide only an insufficient remedy." [20]

The deepest cause of Faust's melancholy is, however, his alienation from any really vital religion. His insatiable hunger for knowledge is not equivalent with any merely positivistic passion for more and more facts. What he wants is the kind of radically ultimate penetration of the total fabric of meaning, the kind of fundamental knowledge of first and last things, which the Christian faith makes accessible. What he had hoped to find somewhere amid the tumultuous and fragmentary world of human life was a point, a still center, around which the broken fragments of experience press into a luminously meaningful pattern. But that pattern is, of course, the pattern of Revelation which Faust's agnosticism can no longer permit him to discern. His awkward way of confessing his alienation from Christianity is to say, "I fear neither Hell nor the Devil." But, he is forced to admit, "in return, I have forfeited all joy." And he has forfeited all joy because, though his problem is essentially a religious problem, he has, by reason of his alienation from his religious tradition, been compelled to seek an answer to it within the terms of secular science—and here no solution of it is to be found. So his last state becomes worse than the first, for he decides to give himself to the dark arts of necromancy and magic. What he cannot have, in other words, by faith he will capture by violence. He is one who would slough off the galling fetters of his finitude in order that he might enter into a direct confrontation with the Mystery of Being and from it wrest by force its hidden secrets. He is not content to "stand before Nature simply as a man"; he is not content to be, in Martin Heidegger's phrase, a finite "being-in-the-world." His finitude has driven him into the profoundest embarrassment, and he is no longer capable of envisaging the possibility that the kind of ultimate wisdom for which he yearns may be attainable only through a series of maneuvers by the analogical imagination whereby the finite world may itself be apprehended as "a glass of vision" into the Ground of Being. So, in his frenetic quest of the Infinite, he has become estranged from the created order of being—which is the order of finitude. And the result is that, in his confusion of spirit, he becomes a kind of aviator, flying directly out of the created order of finite existence into the realm of the Absolute, which he would take by direct assault.

Here, then, we have an exemplification of the pathos arising out of the "exaltation of the imagination in its Cartesian vacuum."[21] The principled contempt for the created order of finite existence which is cultivated in the subjectivistic pursuit of the clear and distinct idea alienates the sensibility from the living body of the world, wherein it can alone gain its proper refreshment, and, when the finite self refuses to know itself as *being-in-the-world,* it must inevitably assume the posture of an angel. This is the case with our major modern hero, and, what is more, the example which is furnished by Goethe's Faust foreshadows a basic predicament of the modern poet himself, whose spiritual history has been, as both M. Maritain and Mr. Tate have seen so clearly, the history of an experiment in angelism.[22]

The first moment in the history of this defection has its beginning perhaps with Lautréamont and is prolonged by a line of modern poets running through the French Surrealists to such writers of the immediate past as Hart Crane and Dylan Thomas; but it is that strange and fascinating child-poet of the French nineteenth century, Arthur Rimbaud, who stands out most sharply for us as representing what is characteristic of the entire tradition—namely, the impulse to escape from the necessity of poetry altogether through the attainment of the kind of mystical gnosis that is conferred upon the hierophant. Rimbaud is, indeed, the very type and example of the modern poet who turns away from the created order of finite existence in order "to force the gates of the mystery which penetrates us and envelops us on all sides."[23] With him modern poetry became a kind of priestly incantation, a method of directly assaulting the Absolute. In the famous "Lettre du Voyant" of 1871, which was addressed to Paul Demeny, he declares:

One must, I say, be a *seer,* make oneself a *seer.*
The poet makes himself a *seer* through a long, a prodigious and rational disordering of *all* the senses. Every form of love, of suffering, of madness; he searches himself, he consumes all the poisons in him, keeping only their quintessences. Ineffable torture in which he will need all his faith and

superhuman strength, the great criminal, the great sickman, the utterly damned, and the supreme Savant! For he arrives at the unknown! Since he has cultivated his soul—richer to begin with than any other! He arrives at the unknown: and even if, half crazed, in the end, he loses the understanding of his visions, he has seen them! Let him croak in his leap into those unutterable and innumerable things: there will come other horrible workers: they will begin at the horizons where he has succumbed.[24]

Here, then, is the poet as angel "who lives more with the invisible than with the visible," [25] the *poète maudit* who seeks an "experience of the blind glitter of nothingness, in which all differences are abolished and all contradictions made one, by virtue of the void, and in which the soul believes it is transferred above everything and enjoys infinite liberty. This is the black mysticism in which poetic knowledge transformed into absolute knowledge finally winds up." [26]

This, now, is the one aspect of what may be called the first moment in the history of the modern poet's angelism, and the other arises out of the doctrine that poetry "should have nothing in view but itself," [27] which Baudelaire elicited from Edgar Poe's two famous essays, "The Philosophy of Composition" and "The Poetic Principle," and which, passing down through Mallarmé and Valéry, led to the effort to produce what has come in France to be called *la poésie pure*. Here we come upon the tradition of those modern writers—of whom the greatest example is perhaps the author of *Finnegans Wake*—who have been "jealous, as it were, of God" [28] and who have wanted themselves to create *ex nihilo* a world of self-sufficient forms, requiring and tolerating no reference to anything beyond themselves. These are the artists who have insisted upon the essential *gratuitousness* of poetry and who, in their effort to be artists and *only* artists, have dedicated themselves to what has often been a frighteningly severe asceticism. They have been acrobats inching their way along a tightrope stretched above the common world of human experience for which they have had no great love. Instead of contemplating the created order of finite existence and then submitting it to the kind of miraculous metamorphosis which poetry accomplishes, they have chosen rather to contemplate the idea of contemplation itself—and to make poetry out of the idea of poetry itself. They have wanted a poetry uncontaminated by the muddy torrents of the world, and their determination has been to produce a poetry that would be a kind of absolute music from which the very last iota of discursive meaning would have been banished. Their purpose was to use words, but to use them in such a way that they would have a meaning thoroughly transferred from the ordinary world to the poetic world. . . . Thus we should end . . . with an intellectual music, made from the poetic content of words in which the main task of the sound was to help obliterate the usual meaning of the words employed, putting a new meaning in its place. This music of meanings resting upon sounds— that is the essential formula of pure poetry.[29]

So radical a segregation of poetry from the world means, of course, the death of poetry, for man is not capable "of producing an absolute mutation, an absolute novelty in the universe."[30] Though men like Mallarmé and Valéry, who undertook this experiment, succeeded in writing some of the greatest poetry of our time, they did so by failing to live up to their doctrine, which, were it really to be adhered to, would condemn the artist to utter defeat. For, as M. Denis de Rougemont has suggested, the poet's task is not to *invent* reality but rather to *discover* it and then to rearrange it in such a way that we may love it more profoundly.[31] He cannot be an angel, and, when he truly understands his vocation, he will not try to be one.

The second major moment in the history of the modern writer's angelism is a chapter in the development not of our poetry but of our fiction—though, in the most generous use of language, it is a moment in the history of modern poetry also, for Mr. Edmund Wilson is, I believe, altogether right in his contention that the technique of modern prose has so absorbed the technique of verse that "If, in writing about 'poetry,' one limits one self to 'poets' who compose in verse, one excludes too much of modern literature."[32]

This second phase of our problem brings before us those poets of the novel in whose work we witness a complete abandonment of the mimetic principle that governs such triumphs of the traditional genre as *Moll Flanders, Madame Bovary, Anna Karenina, The Brothers Karamazov,* and *The Wings of the Dove.* What we confront in the work of writers like Proust and Joyce and Virginia Woolf and Djuna Barnes and Malcolm Lowry is a central tendency in modern fiction— the tendency, that is, to exhibit the created order of existence as being no more than a function of the human consciousness which perceives it. The world into which these writers take us is not—as was the case with Dickens or Stendhal, with Zola or Tolstoi—the public world of which we, together with the writer and his characters, are members; it is rather a world existing autonomously in the consciousness of the discarnate spirits with whom the books of these writers are peopled. In such representative modern books as *Finnegans Wake, To the Light-*

house, Nightwood, and *Under the Volcano* the hegemony of the objective world has been completely broken. The only reality to be discovered is that which flows fitfully and intermittently through the
consciousness of the dramatis personae, and the writer has become, says
Professor Weidlé, borrowing an image from Ortega y Gasset, "like a
man who approaches a window, not to look outside, but to gaze at the
windowpane itself with its tiny defects, the particular shade of the glass
and its relative transparence." [33]

Now I call this particular aspect of the modern imagination "angelic"
because it exemplifies what Mr. Tate has taught us to recognize as
distinctive of the type—namely, the attempt "to disintegrate or to
circumvent the image in the illusory pursuit of essence." [34] The rigor-
ously subjectivistic perspectives of this group of modern writers represent the quest of such a synthesis of the felt intricacies of life as will
reveal the quintessential elixir of consciousness. And it is by no means
difficult to understand why this should have become for the modern
writer a major preoccupation, for one of the most influential currents
in the climate of opinion in which he has lived has been that growing
out of those movements in modern science and philosophy which have
instructed us in the relativity of all our observations of the world and
which have revealed to us a kind of interdependence between the
human observer and the world to which older cosmologies, with their
notions of causation and of dualities of mind and matter, no longer
seem adequate. As every schoolboy knows, we no longer live in the
world of Newton and Laplace but in the world of Planck and Einstein
and Heisenberg in which the fundamental focus of physics is not a fact
and an observer but rather the actual observation occurring in the
observer's prehension of the fact. Indeed, if modern descriptive physics
has convinced us of anything at all, it is of the inseparability of event
and observer and of the utter implausibility of regarding the order in
experience as existing in complete independence of the mind. And so
we should be prepared to welcome versions of experience in the imaginative literature of our time which display "the interanimating richness of the mind which sees and the world which is seen." [35] But what
we have gotten from many great writers of our day is such a reduction
of this complexity as suggests that the order of the world is *merely* a
product of the mind. The perceptive English critic, Mr. Edwin Muir,
has remarked that the contemporary novel—and I am certain that he
has in mind some of the books which I have cited—strikes him at
times "like a sentence that sets out confidently; the grammatical con-

struction is ingenious; we admire the writer's skill in insinuating explanatory and qualifying clauses and all sorts of parentheses; but the sentence remains hanging in the air." [36] And so it must, when the writer's major purpose is no longer that of making us see more profoundly the nature of man's comic and tragic and fateful collisions with the resistant reality of the world but is rather only that of rendering "the continuous rumination of consciousness in its natural and purposeless freedom." [37]

The progress of the literary imagination in our period has, then, brought us to the end of a long experiment—and the end of it is, I suspect, signalized by the agonized consciousness of those Existentialist writers who make agonized consciousness itself into a kind of absolute value and who bring us into what may well be the third and final moment in the history of modern angelism. Notwithstanding their frequent invocation of the dogma that "existence precedes essence," which would seem to put them in opposition to the spirit of Cartesian rationalism, it is, paradoxically, in these writers that the solipsistic idealism of the Cartesian age finally reaches a kind of dead end in the general declaration for absurdity—though, as Mr. Robert Cohn has suggested, it does sometimes appear that M. Sartre has only "revised Descartes's formula to read: 'I belch, therefore I am.' " [38] In such books as Sartre's *La Nausée,* Camus' *Le Mythe de Sisyphe* and *L'Étranger,* Simone de Beauvoir's *Le Sang des autres* and *Pour une morale de l'ambiguité,* and Richard Wright's *The Outsider* we are told that absurdity is the fundamental condition of human life and that life must be lived under the general dispensation of despair. In Sartre's view this fundamental absurdity of existence seems to be a consequence of the absolute incommensurability between *l'être-en-soi* ("being-in-itself") and *l'être-pour-soi* ("being-for-itself"), which, in turn, drives the consciousness or the being *pour-soi* back in upon its own anguished isolation. And the metaphysical malaise into which we are driven by the opaque impenetrability of *things* is nowhere dramatized so memorably as in the person of Antoine Roquentin, the chief character of *La Nausée,* who remains perhaps the archetypal instance of the Existentialist hero and whose story is one of the few really powerful philosophical myths to have emerged from the literature of this century. Here is the Existentialist man whose experience of the disintegration and fragmentariness of life propels him into ennui and whose inability to transcend the viscosity of his own inner life (*le visqueux* is for Sartre a technical term descriptive of the messy disorder of consciousness) and enter into a deeply satisfying intellectual relationship with being *en-soi* produces in him a positive hatred of life. He becomes one whose fundamental sensations are those of nausea and disgust. *Things* begin, indeed, to appear to him to be positively obscene; the very stubbornness with which they persist in being *there,* shamelessly glorying as it were in all of their redolent factuality, comes finally to fill him with horror. It is "the very stuff of things"—whose *thereness* seems to have no link with his own existence and, to that extent, seems to oppose his own inward being—that fills him with distress, because it deepens his sense of the contingency and finitude of his own existence. And Roquentin's plight is that of many another hero in the Existentialist fiction of our day: it is the plight of Sartre's Mathieu, of Camus' Meursault, of Richard Wright's Cross Damon. Oreste remarks at one point in Sartre's play *Les Mouches* that "human life begins on the other side of despair"—which is really for him to say that, in the Existentialist drama, it begins with the individual's discovery of his finitude, of his irremediable ontological solitude. This is the fundamental fact of life, and the individual's life begins with reflection upon this fact, for then it is that it becomes clear to him that the great project of his life must be the quest of such a reintegration into the stable fullness of being as will grant him the ontological integrity that he lacks. But in the Existentialist fiction of our day the hero is never taken beyond the point of this initial realization; he does not know how to go on to fulfillment. He has, as Miss Iris Murdoch has said in her analysis of the Sartrean hero, only "a *dream* of human companionship, but never the experience." [39] He has an intuition of how blessed it would be to be reconciled with the Mystery of Being but never the real experience, for he remains "a solipsistic centre": [40] the world of "I-Thou" remains closed to him. The only victory, it seems, that is possible for him is that which comes with the loss of all hope utterly; and the final movement of his spirit represents a flight into anguish—which appears to be the only attitude to be maintained with dignity by a creature burdened with the curse of having to be *bounded* by other finite presences, between which and oneself there is an ultimate ontological discontinuity whose transcension is impossible so long as one remains confined to the kind of discrete particularity of existence which finitude imposes.

The starting point, at least in our time, of the Christian critic of literature has now, I think, been fully stated. It must, it seems to me, be, first of all, with the assertion that the business of the literary artist is with the natural order of creation—which is the order of finite existence—and then, secondly, it must be with the recognition that the modern writer has, however, had "a very great fear of the finite and the human condition" [41] and has sought to escape from it through various forms of angelism—through magical *gnosis,* through withdrawal into *la poésie pure,* or into the light and airy realms of pure sensibility, or, finally, into the inebriation of *Angst.* Then, once he has taken such a measure as this of where we now stand in the progress of modern literature, the great question, it seems to me, with which the Christian critic must be concerned is the question as to how the modern poet is to be given the courage to glory in our human infirmities and to turn once again to the finite with a sense of wonder and expectancy and with love and a proper adoration.

This is, of course, the point at which the Christian critic's task becomes a philosophical and theological task, for what must be undertaken is such a renewal of the modern poet's ontological vision as will enable him to endure and survive the "boundary situation" into which he has been cast by his anxious ruminations upon all those threatening negativities of finite existence from which he has so desperately wanted to escape. As the Christian critic seeks to define the nature of his mission to the poet in our period, the great question, it seems to me, which he must seek to answer in terms persuasive to the poetic imagination is the question as to the grounds of such a courage as might enable the imagination to affirm the realm of finitude to which we are so indissolubly bound by our human destiny. And in relation to this dimension of his task, he will, I think, as he turns to the history of Christian thought, get his most helpful guidance not from the Thomist but rather from the Augustinian traditions of Christian philosophy. For when he turns, say, to Aquinas, the lesson that he will be taught is, essentially, that the virtue by which the threatening disruptions of finitude are to be faced is not courage but wisdom. It is wisdom, he will be told, that enables the mind to proceed (by way of inference and with the assistance of the principle of causality) from the indigence and incompleteness of finitude to a rational apprehension of the Absolute. Under the dominance of wisdom, in other words, we will submit ourselves to a dialectical process which, as Dr. Langmead Casserley has summed it up, "begins with everyday, external and common-sense things, whose reality is accepted at their face value by all mankind, and then proceeds to demonstrate certain less evident, or perhaps even entirely unknown truths." [42] But surely the Christian critic, by adopting such a tactic, will not be enabled to deliver the modern poetic imagination from that profound embarrassment in the presence of the finite which prevents it from doing its proper work. For this would, in effect, be a philosophical procedure which would bid the modern poet seek stable fullness of Being on the grounds of precisely that about which he is so uncertain, and it would thus only deepen his dilemma. The metaphysics of Thomism must, in other words, be acknowledged as ultimately irrelevant to his spiritual situation.

But when, in quest of the courage that will make possible the acceptance of finitude, the Christian critic turns to the tradition of Augustinian philosophy, he will be led to realize that what he must first of all disclose to the modern poet is that his very distress in the presence of all the limited, incomplete things and events that offer themselves as reality, in so far as it contains implicitly a yearning to behold the infinite, inexhaustible depth of their being and meaning, does itself also contain an awareness of the "moving, restless power" which is "the inner infinity of being" and which informs and sustains all the conditioned and finite forms of existence.[43] For everything that exists, the Augustinian will say, participates in the power of Being-itself, and we are perhaps at no time more deeply aware of what Professor Tillich calls "the Unconditional" than in those moments of our profoundest unsettlement by the indigence and transitoriness of finitude. Indeed, in accordance with this view, it soon begins to appear that faith is itself simply the condition of being grasped by the power of Being-itself, as it affirms itself in and through the structures of finitude—and that the courage that enables the imagination to remain serene in the presence of the finite is rooted in a sense of participation in the ultimate power of Being and in its self-affirmation. And then, since the creative Ground of Being is nowhere for him revealed more transparently than in the New Being made manifest in the New Testament picture of Jesus as the Christ, the Christian critic will be led on to a re-exposition of the Incarnation. For, though the divine Ground of Being cannot be thought of as personal in any limited or existential sense of the term, it cannot at the same time be thought of as less than personal and, apart from the Incarnation, would be characterized by "absolute seclusion" [44] from man's most pressing concerns.

And certainly in Christ we have the most radiantly beautiful example accessible to us of the realm of finitude being approached by the Way of Affirmation. The full significance of the doctrine of the Incarnation is, of course, as Dr. Tillich has reminded us,[45] not properly construed in terms merely of its illumination of the true relation of the finite and the infinite—and yet here surely we have at least one dimension of its significance. For, as the Roman Catholic writer, Fr. William F. Lynch, has so strikingly remarked,

the great qualitative leap into the human way must be found in the New Law with Christ the second Adam as its athlete in the confrontation of the finite. His assumption of finitude is complete and absolute. . . . And this decision, this assumption of the path through the body, is made absolute and irrevocable in the scene of the desert temptations where Christ, tempted to the way of magic and tricks and the direct use of glory and the infinite, chooses the human way.

The great symbols of Christ are evidences of this way. . . . He is the Sun, but the course of this sun is through man. Above all He is a bridegroom . . . and an athlete . . . running with joy . . . through the whole length and depth of the human adventure. . . . He dares more *as a way* than had ever been dared before, marching to the ultimate of the finite. . . . Wherefore he has been exalted and every knee shall bow to him, of all the things that are in heaven or on earth or under the earth. And this is not merely a mark of an external reward for suffering and obedience; it is, be it repeated, the perfect sign and accomplishment of the mysteries or stages of human life, that they are, on a level much more intense than ever before, an intrinsic path to the infinite.[46]

And the great point for the Christian critic is that it is in the athleticism of Christ's penetration of the finite that the literary imagination may find its most instructive norm.

We have now reached the point in our discussion, it seems to me, at which it can be said, by way of concluding this effort at setting forth a kind of prolegomenon to a Christian poetic for our time, that the mission of the Christian critic to the modern poet is one which involves, at bottom, the preparation of a new theonomy, in the sense in which Dr. Tillich has given this term currency in contemporary discussion. The Christian critic, that is to say—when he has truly grasped the genius of the Protestant understanding of the relation of religion and culture—will not, in attempting to redeem the modern poet from the ontological predicament in which he finds himself, urge upon him submission to some enigmatic power *above* existence in obedience to whose alien laws the poet must sacrifice his autonomy. For this is the way of what Dr. Tillich calls "heteronomy," and, though it be the way of Rome, it is not the way a radical Protestantism relates itself to the bearers of culture. The Protestant critic will, instead, seek to disclose to the poet of our time that in the very depth of his ontological confusion there is expressed a sense of the ultimate meaning of existence upon the basis of which he still lives; that in the very seriousness of his sense of separation from the Ground of Being there is expressed a profound intuition of its presence. Thus it is that he will seek to disclose that "Not only he who is in sin but also he who is in doubt is justified through faith"; [47] and thus it is that he will seek to render the artist of our time "open" once more to the Unconditional, not as to something "strange" to the conditioned realities of his experience, but as to that which is their divine Ground. Working in this way and, always tactfully, seeking thus to enter into new *rapprochements* with the artists of our day, it may in time come about that he will be successful in assisting them to face once again the realm of finitude with serenity—"with a sense of wonder and expectancy and with love and a proper adoration," so that their creations may themselves become transparent and be a "glass of vision" through which the ultimate meaning of life may shine for the men of our time.

IV

Man in Recent Literature

AMONG THE BASIC lessons which have been won for us through the researches of modern criticism, there is perhaps none today which figures more largely in our awareness than that which teaches the indispensability of myth and symbol to those procedures of the imagination from which great literature springs. In discussing these questions in his brilliant little book *The Enchaféd Flood,* Mr. W. H. Auden has remarked:

> A constant aesthetic problem for the writer is how to reconcile his desire to include everything, not to leave anything important out, with his desire for an aesthetic whole, that there shall be no irrelevances and loose ends.[1]

That is to say, the artist wants always to convey a vision of the rich plenitude of experience, and yet, if he is not himself to succumb to it, he must have some counterpoise in faith and reason that supports his imagination and that does not leave him too much exposed to the deracinative force of that plenitude. He must have at his disposal, as Mr. Eliot said many years ago in his famous review of James Joyce's *Ulysses,* some means "of controlling, or ordering, of giving a shape and a significance to the immense panorama of . . . anarchy which is contemporary history."[2] There must be operative within his deepest instinctual life a set of *archai,* of first principles, which furnish him a technique of metaphysical and ethical valuation, for without this he cannot bring order and intelligibility to experience: in the traditional Aristotelian language, he cannot produce an imitation; that is to say, he cannot impose a form upon the formless stuff of life itself.

But just here we come upon the reason for the extreme difficulty that has been involved in the creation of art in our time. For modern culture, though it has had many other gifts to bestow upon the artist, has not been able to provide him with the essential thing—"a positive affirmation, the intensity of a great conception," [3] an illuminated point, a still center around which the tumultuous and fragmentary world of contemporary life might be ordered and given meaning. Our poets and novelists have not received from their culture, as Sophocles and Dante and Shakespeare did from theirs, any central myth or body of symbol which, when applied to the modern world, was capable of radical organizing power. The multiplicity of myth or belief—or of what is sometimes called ideology—has often been noted in modern discussion, but by no one with more remarkable concision and vividness than the American poet Karl Shapiro, who, in his *Essay on Rime,* at one point observes:

> So various
> And multifoliate are our breeds of faith
> That we could furnish a herbarium
> With the American specimens alone.
> A choice anthology of a few of these
> Made its appearance just before the war;
> It is an album of philosophies
> Called *I Believe.* The essays it contains
> Have nothing in common but proximity.[4]

And thus it is that Mr. Shapiro provides us with some measure of the degree to which the modern writer has been unable to presuppose agreement between himself and his audience about the ultimate issues of human existence—the kind of agreement, that is, that might furnish his imagination with the premises of its functioning. The modern artist has needed a large and pervasive myth, a frame of traditional values, out of whose logic he might speak with poise and certitude to his contemporaries. But he has had to live and work in a cultural situation in which his position has been very much as that of Dante would have been if he had had himself to elaborate the whole massive structure of Christian myth and symbol before beginning to compose the *Commedia.* This has been the enormous burden and expense not only of literature but of all the other arts in our time—as is indicated, for example, by the restlessness with which Stravinsky in music and Picasso in painting have raced from first one idiom to another: they, too, along with, let us say, Joyce in the novel and Eliot in poetry, have been in search of a myth, of an appropriate mode of vision and of a usable vehicle of communication. Their misfortune has been that of having to live in an age without organic order, presided over by a philosophical and religious pluralism of the most extreme sort. We realize, of course, when we read today Eliot's *The Waste Land* or Joyce's *Finnegans Wake,* when we look at Picasso's *Guernica* mural, or listen to the last quartets of Schoenberg, that this very situation of extreme cultural disorder is capable of stimulating work of great power, and yet we feel, at the same time, that it spells a certain desperate extremity. And when I say this I do not want to be interpreted as implying the pejorative and dismissive judgments which Mr. J. Donald Adams of *The New York Times* often proposes for our edification in his Sunday homilies: I mean only to suggest that the tendencies which these monuments of modern art represent seem, in a way, to promise an exhaustion of any possibilities of further development and to announce a kind of melancholy *eschaton* for the literary life.

Now, in remarking upon the modern artist's search for myth, I have already anticipated the second observation that we must make, which is that, having found his culture to be unstable in its beliefs, he has had to try to supply himself with a usable myth, with a focus of vision whereby the astigmatism to which his age inclines him might be corrected. And immediately many spectacular examples come to mind. There is the example of William Butler Yeats, who, in the process of creating one of the most notable bodies of poetry in this century, amalgamated in the most eccentric fashion the traditions of pagan Ireland and of theosophic Rosicrucianism. There is the even more familiar example in modern poetry of Mr. Eliot, whose great poem of 1922, *The Waste Land,* was erected out of a scaffolding whose sources range all the way from Sir James Frazer to Dante and from the Elizabethans to the French Symbolists. And in the novel we have the dazzling pyrotechnics of Joyce and the highly sophisticated, though by no means wholly successful, effort of Thomas Mann in the *Joseph* stories to rehabilitate Biblical myth. Still much closer to home, we have the examples of Hart Crane in poetry and Thomas Wolfe in the novel, for whom the theme which seemed to promise a subject of mythic proportions was that of America itself.[5] And in the work of many younger poets and novelists of our own day the search for myth is continued and goes on without interruption.

It has, however, during all this time been slowly dawning upon us that the kind of myth for which the modern writer has striven is not something that can be created by an act of will. Vital myth and symbol are not produced by fiat. They are, rather, the expressions of a deep sense of organic unity that, gathering over a long period of time, binds a people together with ties of sympathy and of fellow feeling, and they become the means whereby that people is united, as Professor Philip Wheelwright has said, "with the unplumbed Mystery from which mankind is sprung and without reference to which the radical signifi-cance of things goes to pot." [6] And when the mythical consciousness has been lost—as it has been very largely lost to us through the corrod-ing acids of modernity, the acids of behaviorism and instrumentalism and semantic positivism and all the other secular and naturalistic heresies of the modern world—when the mythical consciousness has been lost, the poet is without that common background of transcen-dental reference by which the imaginative faculties of his readers and of himself are oriented and so brought into profounder rapport than would otherwise have been possible. In such a situation the writer must be content either with turning inward upon himself and report-ing on his own malaise or simply with making the barest of indicative statements about his environing world. In the one case we have the literature of pure sensibility—the novel, say, in the hands of André Gide or Virginia Woolf—and in the other case we have the literature of naturalistic metajournalism, the novels of Farrell and Dos Passos or of the young postwar Americans, Norman Mailer and James Jones.

Neither is, of course, today quite satisfactory. The purveyors of pure sensibility do not satisfy us because, our generation having inherited in the past thirty years not the world of John Dewey but that of Nietzsche, "the artist's estrangement is no longer a phenomenon unique but rather something shared." [7] And so we expect our writers, when they write out of their own discomforts, to do so in such a way as to suggest a recognition on their part of their implication in a col-lective tragedy. We look to them for some hint of how the self-encyst-ment of the ego may be broken and we may gain release from the awful prison of our private fantasies into a public world of fellowship and community. We want them to give us some sense of man as Man, and thereby to give us a presentiment of abiding values beyond the despair of our age. But we do not get this in the novels of Proust and Virginia Woolf, of Italo Svevo and André Gide, and so there comes a time when we feel that we must refuse their enchantments.

The literary naturalists, on the other hand, do not satisfy us because, in their subversive way, they co-operate with all the impulses of a secular culture to disenthrone the imagination, whether in its aesthetic or in its religious phases, in the interest of "the scientific observation of fact." The names of men like Dreiser and Dos Passos, Farrell and the early Steinbeck, or, among younger writers, Norman Mailer and James Jones put us in mind of that current in our literature which has wanted to give us the illusion of history by eradicating the distinction between life and art and by giving us so large a slice of the crude, raw stuff of life as to make us forget when we read their novels that we are, after all, reading a work of fiction. And thus by banishing themselves from their books and muffling their own voices, in the manner of the competent photographer or reporter, they have, as Mr. Lionel Trilling has said, only "reinforced the faceless hostility of the world and have tended to teach us that we ourselves are not creative agents and that we have no voice, no tone, no style, no significant existence." [8] But surely, as Mr. Trilling goes on to say in his book, *The Liberal Imagination,* "what we need is the opposite of this, the opportunity to identify ourselves with a mind that willingly admits that it is a mind and does not pretend that it is History or Events or the World but only a mind thinking and planning—possibly planning our escape." [9]

What is perhaps at the root of our dissatisfaction with both the literature of pure sensibility and the literature of naturalism is their failure to give us what the naturalists have unsuccessfully tried to furnish—namely, a clarified and deepened vision of history. The distinguished French man of letters, M. Jean-Paul Sartre, tells us that we are living through what he calls an "extreme situation," by which, presumably, he means to bring us up short against the great and sobering fact of our time—which is that tidal forces "powerful enough to . . . nullify the bequest of centuries" [10] are today sweeping across the earth and thundering upon the door of our children's future: he means to tell us that our crisis is radical and that we have been brought to bay at the extremity of the human situation. And in such a world, where the fire is put out and the sun is lost, what little light remains must be used for the quest of the one thing needful, and imaginative literature must, therefore, be a way of reading the human condition and a counterpoise to chaos, for that is what our time requires. This is not, of course, to say that our writers must be "public health officers, criers of economic and political cures," as Diana Trilling has said we have sometimes mistakenly insisted that they be.[11] In their office as "renovators of the spirit," their one task is to be "spokesmen for the self and the self's mysterious possibilities" [12] and, in the present time, to seize upon the crises and distempers of modern history as means for the conveyance to us of a deeper knowledge of ourselves and of what is sometimes called our "boundary situation." And in spite of all the unfortunate excrescences that attach to M. Sartre's theory of "engaged literature," it is, I think, the chief merit of that doctrine to make this assertion. In speaking of his own literary generation in France, he remarks upon the "historicity" that has flowed in upon the pages of the books they have written and says:

we are Jansenists because the age has made us such, and insofar as it has made us touch our limits I shall say that we are all metaphysical writers. I think that many among us would deny this designation or would not accept it without reservations, but this is the result of a misunderstanding. For metaphysics is not a sterile discussion about abstract notions which have nothing to do with experience. It is a living effort to embrace from within the human condition in its totality.

Forced by circumstances to discover the pressure of history, as Torricelli discovered atmospheric pressure, and tossed by the cruelty of the time into that forlornness from where one can see our condition as man to the very limit, to the absurd, to the night of unknowingness, we have a task for which we may not be strong enough. . . . It is to create a literature which unites and reconciles the metaphysical absolute and the relativity of the historical fact, and which I shall call, for want of a better name, the literature of great circumstances.[13]

But this—namely, a literature of great circumstances—is precisely what we have not obtained from either the creators of the literature of pure sensibility or from the modern naturalists: in the one case because the writer has not been able to cross-question himself out of his solipsism into an awareness of the public world of which both he and his readers are living members; in the other case because a fiction committed to the mere enumeration of social and political detail, though it may reproduce the disorder of the contemporary world, is incapable of giving its drama the dimension of tragic grandeur. This is perhaps to say that neither current within our recent literature has possessed an adequate myth or body of symbol whereby, in Mr. Eliot's words, "a shape and a significance" might be given "to the immense panorama of . . . anarchy which is contemporary history."

But if imaginative literature is to engage itself profoundly with the historical drama of our time, it must somehow lay hold of new myths and symbols that are appropriate correlatives of that drama, and the writers who move us most deeply today are, I believe, those in whom we feel the mythmaking imagination to be most powerfully at work. And in this connection I am impelled to recall the testimony of many young men who saw active service during the past war and who have told me of the excitement with which they rediscovered, somewhere in the Pacific or in Europe, often in a USO library, Herman Melville's *Moby Dick*. The voyage of that old monomaniac Captain Ahab and his fellow pilgrims gave these young soldiers, they have told me, a kind of release: that is, the journey of Ahab's strange crew in their small bark over the uncharted waters of the deep gave these young men a sense of what their situation then really was and of what man's condition in the world has always been; as they considered the infernal land upon which they fought and the storm-tossed seas over which the *Pequod* rolled, they found, as Melville had predicted, a strange analogy to something in themselves. And the late F. O. Matthiessen similarly recalled in his journal, *From the Heart of Europe,* the many young American soldiers who told him after the war of the release that they were given by Henry James while they were in the army. "They had felt a great need," said Matthiessen, "during the unrelenting outwardness of those years, for his kind of inwardness, for his kind of order as a bulwark against disorder." [14]

Here, then, is evidence of how intense a preoccupation among sensitive young people of our day is the search for new symbols and myths, and thus it is not at all surprising that this is what we value most highly in the literature of the recent past and in the literature of our own period. So it is perhaps one of the most important cultural inquiries that can be made at the moment to ask what are some of the more pervasive myths or patterns of symbolic statement about the human condition discernible in contemporary literature. And there are four that I should like briefly to discuss. There are, of course, others, and these that I shall treat might be differently named, but I shall call them the Myth of the Isolato, the Myth of Hell, the Myth of Voyage, and the Myth of Sanctity. [15] The form of our excursion will, in other words, resemble that of Dante's *Commedia:* we shall begin in "the dark wood," and we shall end with bliss, of which, to be sure, there is not a great deal in contemporary literature; and such as there is does not perhaps resemble very greatly the bliss of the *Paradiso*. But, nevertheless, if justice is to be done to the modern writer's testimony, we must attend not only to his anatomy of melancholy but also, finally, to his anatomy of blessedness.

Our most abiding impression, however, of the report on contemporary man's spiritual estate that the literature of our period submits is that his condition is described in terms of isolation and estrangement.

In the earlier part of Melville's *Moby Dick* there occur two chapters which are devoted to a description of the men who composed Captain Ahab's crew, and toward the close of the second of these two chapters Melville says: "They were nearly all Islanders in the Pequod, *Isolatoes* too, I call such, not acknowledging the common continent of men, but each *Isolato* living on a separate continent of his own." And it has been with this sentence in mind that I have called the first of the symbolic patterns in modern literature to which we now turn the Myth of the Isolato. Mr. William Faulkner tells us of Joe Christmas, the mulatto protagonist of *Light in August,* that "there was something definitely rootless about him, as though no town nor city was his, no street, no walls, no square of earth his home. And . . . he carried his knowledge with him always as though it were a banner, with a quality ruthless, lonely and almost proud." The same might also be said of Conrad's Heyst in *Victory,* of Joyce's Bloom in *Ulysses,* of Graham Greene's Pinkie in *Brighton Rock,* and of Robert Penn Warren's Jeremiah Beaumont in *World Enough and Time.* For the image of man that recurs most frequently in these and many of the other memorable books of our time is the image of man as *Isolato,* of the individual as "living on a separate continent of his own." That this emphasis upon alienation and lostness should be a hallmark of our literature is easily explained by reference to reasons which it is beyond our purview here to explore. The fundamental explanation is doubtless that the shape of the modern writer's imagination has been but an analogue of the historical situation in which he has found himself. He has lived in a world struck through by profound social and political dislocation, and he has also, more often than not, lived in urban communities the primary quality of whose life has been impersonality and uprootedness from the soil, from the family, and from all those other basic organic unities of life from which the spirit of man derives its deepest nourishment.[16] Indeed, it is significant that the City—which is one of the most recurrent symbols in modern fiction—is, in Joyce's *Ulysses,* in Dos Passos's *Manhattan Transfer,* in Albert Camus's *The Plague,* an image of despair, as it is in Isaiah and Jeremiah.[17] So it should not, therefore, be at all surprising that the sense of deracination, of spiritual insecurity, and the preoccupation with the theme of moral isolation are pervasive throughout the work of the more serious writers of our day. Their characters are, as a rule, homeless derelicts in search of self-definition and the Mystery of Being.

It is perhaps in the novels of Franz Kafka (who, it has often been said, bears much the same relation to our age that Dante, Shakespeare, and Goethe bore to theirs) that we get the most archetypal presentation of the contemporary hero. His is the religious consciousness of the age —by which I mean what Mr. Wallace Fowlie means when he makes a similar claim for the French painter Rouault: I mean that Kafka's is "a mind which contains the terrors and nightmares of the age which most of us can't face." [18] What is perhaps first to be remarked upon is the atmosphere of isolation that pervades his books, enveloping and conditioning the destiny of his hero who holds no definite position in the world and whose name, in one case, consists only of a single letter. At the center of his novels there is always the single individual, the lonely and uprooted "Isolato," for whom there is no fixed abode and who, in becoming a kind of clown, grows "more conscious of his center, of his distance from God, of the mechanical awkwardness of his gestures, of the dizzying somersaults his spirit performs before the revolving universe and the eternal peace of God." [19] In *The Castle,* for example, K. arrives one night in the Village, to which he believes himself to have been called to practice the profession of Land Surveyor. But he discovers after his arrival that there is no prepared place for him and that, as the life of the Village is controlled by the Castle which is situated on a hill above the little hamlet, in order to remain there he must secure a special dispensation from the Castle officials. The novel becomes, then, the story of his progress toward this end which will be his salvation. But the progress is precisely the thing that remains always in question and that is the chief problem. K.'s goal is clear: it is acceptance. And we do not doubt the reality of a road that leads to this goal. But how to discover this road and, in the absence of any clearly defined signs, how to remain on it, once it is discovered—these are the chief problems. K. has no good guide, such as Dante had in Virgil, and so he must discover everything for himself. All the accumulated lore of the folk and even his own intuitions appear to be unreliable. He is the prototype of the modern man who, as Mr. Auden has well said, no longer being supported by a living tradition, must "do deliberately for himself what in previous ages had been done for him by family, custom, Church, and State—namely, the choice of the principles and presuppositions in terms of which he can make sense of his experience." [20] Of course, K. never really gets anywhere: he never succeeds in getting from the Castle an unequivocal declaration of his right to remain in the Village. But, paradoxically, this is his triumph, his assurance that he is on the right road; for were

he to become convinced of having achieved some simple *modus
vivendi* between himself and the Castle, we should know that he had
failed. He must, that is, as St. Augustine advised, delight to find God
in failing to find Him, because (as Mr. Auden remarked a few years
ago on the occasion of a laymen's Sunday service in a New York
Episcopal church), though "our dominant experience [today] is of
God's absence, of His distance . . . for our time, the distance of God
may be something He wishes us to learn."

"The distance of God"—this might, indeed, be regarded as a major
lesson of many of the most memorable books of our time, of Céline's
Journey to the End of Night, of Djuna Barnes's *Nightwood,* of Na-
thanael West's *Miss Lonelyhearts,* of Robert Penn Warren's *World
Enough and Time,* and of André Malraux's *The Walnut Trees of
Altenburg.* Joseph Conrad tells us in *Nostromo* that "Solitude from
mere outward condition of existence becomes very swiftly a state of
soul in which the affectations of irony and skepticism have no place.
It takes possession of the mind, and drives forth the thought into the
exile of utter unbelief." And it is this dialectical unfolding which is
exhibited in a great deal of modern literature. So it is no wonder, then,
that we have been made familiar with Hell—which is but the moment
in which man, in the arrest of his melancholy, makes the discovery
that he is something less than what he should be. Of the personae
in his early novels, in whom he would have us see ourselves, Mr.
Graham Greene has said more than once, "Hell lay about them in their
infancy," and Kate Farrant remarks at one point in Mr. Greene's
England Made Me:

> "We're all thieves. . . . Stealing a livelihood here and there and every-
> where, giving nothing back. . . . No brotherhood in our boat. Only who
> can cut the biggest dash and who can swim."

"It is the moment of the whirlpool," says the poet Archibald Fleming,
"moment/Of the abyss where all things stream"[21]—the moment in
which we are surprised to learn "That Death so great a legion had
undone."[22] And so M. Sartre puts the three characters in his play *No
Exit* in Hell, which is portrayed as a Second Empire furnished living
room. Their sentence condemns them to eternal wakefulness in a room
lit by a glaring light which will never go out, and their condition is
infernal, we are given to understand, because each is utterly out of
harmony with the others. Their situation is summed up at the end of
the play by Garcin, the male member of the trio, who declares: "Hell

is—other people!" And, finally, the metaphysical fables of, let us say, Robert Penn Warren, together with the moral fables of Sartre, are converted into political terms by a writer like George Orwell, so that in *Nineteen Eighty-Four* we are given still another abstract for a contemporary Inferno. Indeed, it is as if many of the representative writers of our time by an act of general consent had agreed to recreate "the myth of the land blighted by a curse, the land awaiting redemption by water." Toward the close of *The Waste Land* Mr. Eliot declares: "These fragments I have shored against my ruins," and this line might be given general application, for it is the image of "ruins" that is the residue in the mind after its encounter with a central strain in modern literature. And nowhere, perhaps, does the Myth of Hell have a more vivid and impressive life than in the novels of Mr. William Faulkner, whose greatness in the things of the imagination our generation is only beginning to discover.

An objection might, of course, be raised to the introduction of Mr. Faulkner into the pattern of our argument at this point, for it might be said that the literature with which we are dealing here is an international literature in the sense that the experience which it documents has become international, as we have become an international people. But, so the argument might run, there is no major figure in modern literature who has been more bound to a special locale than Mr. Faulkner. And in a sense this is true, for, in the many wonderful books that have been coming from his pen during the past thirty years, he has given us, first of all, as Mr. Malcolm Cowley has argued,[23] a connected story of the mythical kingdom that forms the landscape of his books and that he calls Yoknapatawpha County, Mississippi; and then he has gone on to offer this story as a legend not only of the patch of land in Mississippi in which he has his own familial roots but of all the deep South. His myth has, in other words, been the Southern myth which has as its subject the fate of a ravaged land. In his fine book on Faulkner Mr. Irving Howe presents the following notation of this myth: he says:

The homeland—so the story goes—had proudly insisted that it alone should determine its destiny; provoked into a war impossible to win, it had nevertheless fought to its last strength, and had fought this war with a reckless gallantry and a superb heroism that, as Faulkner might say, made of its defeat not a shame but almost a vindication. But the homeland fell, and from this fall came misery and squalor: the ravaging by the conquerors, the loss of faith among the descendants of the defeated, and the rise of a new breed of faceless men who would batten on their neighbors' humiliation.[24]

And the old South, says Mr. Howe, over which the myth

chants in threnody is an ideal image—a buried city, Allen Tate has called it. Both the violence and the poignancy with which this ideal image have been employed suggest an awareness that the buried city can never be found.[25]

Mr. Faulkner's relation to this myth is, of course, highly complicated, and it can by no means be responsibly construed as having yielded, on his part, any simple program of Southern apologetics. And though the myth furnishes an excellent platform from which to launch into the world of *The Sound and the Fury, As I Lay Dying, Light in August,* and *Absalom, Absalom!,* we should not allow our preoccupation with it to betray us into an overemphasis upon the Southern elements in his writing. For, though his materials derive from the American South, his essential comment is upon issues of human existence that are common to the modern world.

The universe that Mr. Faulkner has created is, one feels, a world contaminated, fundamentally, by something like Original Sin. It is a world "peopled by young men like fallen angels, and of a meteoric violence like that of fallen angels, beyond heaven or hell and partaking of both: doomed immortality and immortal doom" (*Sartoris*). Indeed, the words to which he returns again and again for descriptive purposes, with a kind of desperate automatism, are "tragic," "inexorable," "intractable," and "outrage." He frequently speaks of "the tragic and inevitable land," "the ancient and tragic womb of the world," and one night, as Byron Bunch of *Light in August* enters the house of the Reverend Gail Hightower and notices the thick, musty smell of "the stale, mankept house," it occurs to him that this is "the odor of goodness. Of course," he reflects, "it would smell bad to us that are bad and sinful." Quentin McCaslin says to his sister in *The Sound and the Fury:* ". . . there's a curse on us it's not our fault," and thus he takes us directly to what is "the basic mold of life for Faulkner's characters." [26] And in this connection it is significant that Mr. Faulkner reminds us, in the Appendix which he prepared for the Modern Library edition of *The Sound and the Fury,* of Ikkemotubbe, the Indian chieftain who, when he went to New Orleans, was called *du Homme* but who, being "himself a man of wit and imagination as well as a shrewd judge of character, including his own, carried [it] one step further and anglicised it to 'Doom.' " The world, in fact, through which Mr. Faulkner's people move is a doomed and accursed place in which man has to bear heavy burdens and in which, as Hightower suggests, he has to perform, to engender, so much more than he can or should have to bear, in order to discover that he can bear anything at all.

All of this is, of course, written out in terms of the moral history of the South—which means that Mr. Faulkner, especially as he is at once a deeply committed and deeply skeptical member of that community, occupies an unusually favorable standpoint from which to view the larger community of the modern world. For it is the habit of the white Southerner who possesses a sense of history to look backward with regretful nostalgia toward "old ghost times" in which life was on occasion graced by a kind of honor, a kind of code, a kind of beauty and order, which it has not often attained in the subsequent development of American society. But then, in the degree to which the conscience of the Southern white man is sensitive, he is also mindful of the sin by which those old times were accursed, of the tragic injustice inherent in them that assumed the form of Negro slavery, of the social tradition that has bequeathed to the children of the slaves such heavy burdens of deprivation and inequity. And so he looks forward to the community's expiation of its guilt, to the time when, as Mr. Faulkner says in *Intruder in the Dust,* the Negro can "shoot a white man in the back with the same impunity to lynchrope or gasoline as a white man," when he can "vote anywhen and anywhere a white man can and send his children to the same school anywhere the white man's children go and travel anywhere the white man travels as the white man does it." But the present moment is suspended between the "old ghost times" and this desired future, and thus it becomes possible for the Southern artist to achieve, as Mr. Faulkner has done, a profound realization of the central predicament of modern man which is that of having to live, as Dr. Reinhold Niebuhr has said, in an "age between the ages" [27] in which a new era of justice and order awaits to be born but in which there is not strength to bring forth. "Thus saith Hezekiah, This day is a day of trouble, and of rebuke, and blasphemy: for the children are come to the birth, and there is not strength to bring forth" (II Kings 19:3).

Now the observations that we have been making have, essentially, been calculated to suggest that the modern writer has often wanted to lead us toward a deeper imaginative seizure of the infernal realities of our time, so that we might be brought nearer "New styles of architecture, a change of heart."[28] And in so doing he has often felt it necessary to use violence and melodrama as instruments for awakening his age out of its lethargies, for destroying its specious securities and revealing its underlying nightmare and tragedy. He has wanted to "prohibit sharply the rehearsed response"[29] and to exhibit the world itself, in all of its degradation, as the country wherein man's spiritual origin is to be rediscovered. His purpose has, however, been sometimes misunderstood, and the complaint has been—very often, indeed, in the case of Mr. Faulkner—that his work is too negative in tone, that its excitation of terror is too radical, and we have sometimes even made the mistake of supposing that the sordid phenomena of dilapidation upon which he has focused have been simply analogues of his own spiritual condition, completely forgetting that more often than not the shape of his imagination has been a reflection of the tragically disordered world in which he has lived. But what we have always to remember is that modern literature, even in its most negative phases, need not be utterly spendthrift of hope and health. For, as men so different from each other as Aristotle and Jeremiah knew, the human heart may on occasion be resurrected through terror. And that is the noble aim which the artist of our day has often had in view. This is doubtless the explanation of the radically subversive quality in such modern texts as Ignazio Silone's *Bread and Wine,* Sartre's trilogy *Les Chemins de la Liberté,* W. H. Auden's *The Age of Anxiety,* Robert Lowell's *Lord Weary's Castle,* and Ralph Ellison's *Invisible Man.* The writer has wanted, if I may paraphrase a line from Mr. Faulkner's Nobel Prize Award speech at Stockholm, to make our griefs grieve on universal bones, and to leave us with scars, for to be unscarred amidst the wreckage and catastrophe of our time is to be less than human. "The abyss destroys; the abyss exalts; descend that you may be saved. The enemy we conquer is the enemy we embrace and love." "Then one fine day," says the American writer Henry Miller, "we will burst the belt and we will be out—in a bright new realm, the unhistorical realm when art will have disappeared entirely because life itself will have become an art." And it is along the exposed and uncharted paths which lead to this "brave new world" that our great writers have sought to make us travel. They have wanted us, in other words, to undertake a journey —sometimes through the self and sometimes through the world—and thus it becomes possible to denominate as a third pattern of symbolic statement in contemporary literature what I have called the Myth of Voyage.

Mr. Auden, in an essay on Kafka, has discussed various versions in the history of literature of the Myth of Voyage or of what he calls "the Quest." He distinguishes there between the Fairy Story, whose hero goes out in quest of some sacred object and succeeds because he does not overestimate his gifts and because he is always willing to help even those who it would seem could not possibly assist him, yet, as it turns out, are precisely the ones who can; the Grail Story, in which the hero attains the sacred object because, being strengthened by the supernatural gift of grace, he withstands the temptation to give up the search for the sake of immediate pleasure; the Dream Quest, in which the purpose of the journey is not a sacred object but spiritual knowledge which the dreamer attains, if at all, by divine grace; and the "Pilgrim's Progress," which is, he says,

no longer a special journey within life, like the quest for the Grail or the Dream Journey, but earthly life itself from birth to death. The goal is salvation, and though this is a universal goal, for everyone has to take the journey, each journey is unique. . . . The Way may be difficult but it is not deceptive, so long as one keeps the goal clearly in mind and never stops willing to get there.[30]

Now it is this final type of voyage—"the journey of life itself which all must take, since its aim is salvation" [31]—that is a frequent symbol in modern literature. And since it is often "no journey to a land we know," the American poet Louise Bogan urges us:

> Bend to the chart, in the extinguished night
> Mariners! Make way slowly; stay from sleep;
> That we may have short respite from such light.
> And learn, with joy, the gulf, the vast, the deep.[32]

But however strange the country into which the pilgrim travels, it is, nevertheless, the pattern of pilgrimage, of voyage, which the modern writer has employed again and again by way of suggesting the stratagem whereby Yeats's "bitter furies of complexity" [33] are to be broken. This voyage is, as Professor Stanley Hopper has reminded us, "not outward, but inward";[34] and though Conrad's Razumov, Kafka's Joseph K., Joyce's Stephen Dedalus, and Sartre's Mathieu journey through the world, the world that contains them is the soulscape of contemporary man—which they explore, over all its devious terrain, in their search for "The Good Place." [35]

Toward the end of his life Thomas Wolfe came to realize that *You Can't Go Home Again,* and in the same year that Wolfe's book appeared posthumously (1940) Mr. Eliot was telling us in "The Dry Salvages" to "fare forward, voyagers." And it is to that version of the Myth of Voyage which is to be found in his later poetry that I want now briefly to turn. His delineation is perhaps not typical, as doubtless no Christian poet's could be in our present cultural situation; but he has seemed to so many of us to be, as the Quakers say, speaking to the human condition as few modern writers have done, and so his is a good contemporary voice to listen to.

In setting forth the way by which the soul journeys toward "the completion of its partial ecstasy./The resolution of its partial horror," [36] Mr. Eliot's use of the sixteenth-century Spanish mystic, St. John of the Cross, is decisive, for it is St. John's doctrine of the *via negativa* around which much of his later work is organized. St. John tells us in *The Ascent of Mt. Carmel* that

there are three reasons for which this journey made by the soul to union with God is called night. The first has to do with the point from which the soul goes forth, for it has gradually to deprive itself of desire for all the worldly things which it possessed, by denying them to itself; the which denial and deprivation are, as it were, night to all the senses of man. The second reason has to do with the mean, or the road along which the soul must travel to this union—that is, faith, which is likewise as dark as night to the understanding. The third has to do with the point to which it travels—namely God, Who, equally, is dark night to the soul in this life. These three nights must pass through the soul,—or rather, the soul must pass through them—in order that it may come to Divine union with God.[37]

And it is this Negative Way which is everywhere the presupposition of Mr. Eliot's poetry of the past twenty-five years. We find it adumbrated in the opening lines of "Ash Wednesday," as the speaker voices his recognition that the impotence and velleity must be suffered without lament; and Harry Monchensy in *The Family Reunion* comes finally to decide that "from a world of insanity" one can only go

> Somewhere on the other side of despair.
> To the worship in the desert, the thirst and deprivation,
> A stony sanctuary and a primitive altar,
> The heat of the sun and the icy vigil . . .[38]

It gains explicit statement in the opening lines of "Burnt Norton":

> Descend lower, descend only
> Into the world of perpetual solitude,

World not world, but that which is not world,
Internal darkness, deprivation
And destitution of all property,
Desiccation of the world of sense,
Evacuation of the world of fancy,
Inoperancy of the world of spirit;
This is the one way, and the other
Is the same . . .[39]

And in the second of the *Quartets,* "East Coker," the tourist who seeks the "strait way" of the "dark night of the spirit" is given "a list of guidebook maxims": [40]

In order to arrive there,
To arrive where you are, to get from where you are not,
You must go by a way wherein there is no ecstasy.
In order to arrive at what you do not know
You must go by a way which is the way of ignorance.
In order to possess what you do not possess
You must go by the way of dispossession.
In order to arrive at what you are not
You must go through the way in which you are not.[41]

The way that leads toward health and blessedness involves, in other words, first of all, a descent into those dark and deep places of the soul which Dante, under Virgil's tutelage, takes us through in the first *cantica* of his poem. We must discover, yes, as Mr. Auden says, how,

Ubiquitous within the bond
Of one impoverishing sky,
Vast spiritual disorders lie.[42]

But we must also discover what wretchedness there is within "Our parish of immediacy," [43] for the patient cannot be cured until he acknowledges that he is ill, and this acknowledgment becomes possible only after we have journeyed beyond the "hither" world of ignorant complacency into the "nether" world of dread and trembling. What is required is humility:

The only wisdom we can hope to acquire
Is the wisdom of humility . . .[44]

The necessary attitude is that of Rilke's "deeply-kneeling man," for thereby alone may the pilgrim behold the Blessed Face and hear the Voice. So

"Fare forward, you who think that you are voyaging;
You are not those who saw the harbour
Receding, or those who will disembark.
Here between the hither and the farther shore
While time is withdrawn, consider the future
And the past with an equal mind.
At the moment which is not of action or inaction
You can receive this: 'on whatever sphere of being
The mind of a man may be intent
At the time of death'—that is the one action . . .
Which shall fructify in the lives of others:
And do not think of the fruit of action.
Fare forward. . . ."

        Not fare well,
But fare forward, voyagers.[45]

"Our principal concern at the present moment," declared T. E.
Hulme over forty years ago, "should be the re-establishment of the
temper or disposition of mind which can look at a *gap* or chasm without shuddering." [46] And it is this charismatic power that many of the
great seers of our time have coveted for us and believed could be won
only by a plunge into our "voided interiority." [47] Joseph Conrad told
us many years ago: "In the destructive element immerse. That is the
way"; and the psychologist Carl Jung has spoken of the necessity of a
descent into the "great waters" of the unconscious. Mr. Auden assures
us that the "Pilgrim Way" leads to "the Abyss," and countless other
modern writers might be cited who think of the contemporary hero as
one who undertakes a voyage or journey into a "nether" world. But
"As from true contemplation the soul inevitably returns to action, so
from the 'nether' she returns to a 'hither' world regenerated in her
regenerate vision." [48] And so we must now finally turn to what I have
called the Myth of Sanctity in contemporary literature.

Many years ago Mr. Eliot, in his celebrated essay on Dante, told us
that "It is apparently easier to accept damnation as poetic material than
purgation or beatitude; less is involved," he said, "that is strange to the
modern mind." [49] And so, therefore, partly no doubt because of my
own partial affliction with this modern insensibility and partly because
of the paucity of descriptions of blessedness in contemporary writing,
I shall devote only the briefest word to this final pattern. It is, to be
sure, a figure in the carpet of modern literature—though, unfor-
tunately, perhaps for the reason Mr. Eliot suggests, it is a relatively

minor figure. More than thirty years ago the late Bernard Shaw, in the greatest play of his career, pondered the mystery of sanctity in *St. Joan,* and earlier still the French poet Charles Péguy was also meditating upon *Le Mystère de la charité de Jeanne d'Arc.* More recently in his play of 1935, *Murder in the Cathedral,* and in his play of 1950, *The Cocktail Party,* Mr. Eliot himself has been coming to grips with this tremendous theme. Nor have the poets and dramatists been alone in this: the English novelist Mr. Graham Greene, in two of his finest books, *The Heart of the Matter* and *The End of the Affair,* has shared their preoccupation; and his fellow craftsman in the novel in France, the late Georges Bernanos, in such books as *Sous le Soleil de Satan* and *Journal d'un curé de campagne,* returned again and again to the mysteries of holiness and beatitude. But these writers, in their concern with this theme, have been a small minority, for the beauty of holiness has only rarely been exhibited by the principal artists of our period. This is not at all to say, however, that Joyce and Kafka and Faulkner have not taken us into the precincts of the world of love: it is only to say that it has been their more usual habit to reveal that world to us through the nocturnal glow of our own tragic time. They have wanted to give us myths and symbols of truth. And if they have succeeded, there may be coming a day not far hence when we may once again be given images of beauty.

V

The Personal Principle: A Conspectus
of the Poetic and
Religious Vision at the Present Time

THERE IS A sense in which I believe it is possible to regard the period through which we are living today as an age of vigil, and nowhere has this aspect of our situation been more affectingly dramatized than in Samuel Beckett's remarkable play *Waiting for Godot*, to which many of us lately have found ourselves returning again and again to meditate upon its profound testimony about the condition of man in our time.

Like such guidebooks for the modern tourist as Kafka's *The Castle*, Auden's *The Age of Anxiety*, and Sartre's *No Exit*, the form of Mr. Beckett's play is characterized by a kind of great and terrible simplicity. Two dirty, stinking, mud-caked tramps, Estragon and Vladimir, come before us and take up their stand under a withered tree on an untraveled road to wait for someone called Godot. They hungrily nibble on scraps of carrots and turnips, as they scratch their vermin-infested bodies and gaze into the vacant, unconsoling sky. And, as they sit and walk about under the tree, they talk: Estragon suggests to Vladimir that they try to converse with each other calmly: "It's so we won't think," he says: "It's so we won't hear. . . . All the dead voices." And when Vladimir asks what the voices say, Estragon replies: "They talk about their lives. . . . They have to talk about it." Vladimir quickly understands and says: "To have lived is not enough for them. . . . To be dead is not enough for them." And Estragon concurs, saying, yes, "It's not sufficient. . . . They have to talk about it."

So, like the dead, these two raffish scamps talk to each other about their lives—sometimes growing angry and quarreling and very nearly fighting each other; but then they will become reconciled, and they will tenderly embrace each other and tell jokes and even laugh. But when they break into laughter, they immediately stifle it, reminding each other that no longer must they dare to laugh. Sometimes they try to remember what they did yesterday, but the past cannot be summoned up with any assurance of clarity. And when they consider what they should do today, they regularly reach the conclusion that nothing is to be done except to wait for Godot. On one occasion it occurs to Estragon to wonder what exactly they did ask Godot for. "Oh . . . Nothing very definite," Vladimir replies. But then Estragon recalls, and he says: "A kind of prayer. . . . A vague supplication." "Precisely," replies Vladimir, but then he reminds Estragon that Godot really promised nothing at all. And when Estragon asks, with a touch of indignation, "Where do we come in?" (meaning "have they no rights at all? can they not expect at least some consideration?"), Vladimir astringently replies: "Come in? On our hands and knees. . . . Your Worship wishes to assert his prerogatives? . . . You'd make me laugh if it wasn't prohibited."

Vladimir's imagination is obsessed by the drama that was enacted long years ago outside the city walls on Golgotha, and he cannot forget the tradition that one of the two thieves crucified with Christ was saved. "It's a reasonable percentage," he says, and he suggests to Estragon that they too may be as lucky, if Godot comes. So, huddling together, they continue to wait by the withered tree, there where Godot had said that he would meet them.

After a time the colloquy between the two tramps is interrupted by the appearance of Pozzo and his slave Lucky. Pozzo is a humorless and imperious nobleman who believes that he is made "in God's image" and who treats his slave with unconscionable cruelty. He refers to Lucky as a pig and torments him with such relish that Estragon calls him a swine. But from Lucky, though he is constantly flogged and opprobriated, there comes not a single murmur of protest. He is sullen and unhappy and without hope, but he remains silent, for his spirit has been so cowed by his master until he is no longer sufficiently human to make the venture of communication: he is only a robot who dances when he is told to dance and who, when he is ordered by Pozzo to entertain Estragon and Vladimir by providing an exhibition of "thinking," can only gurgle out a long, senseless, Joycean tirade. Pozzo and Lucky are not seeking Godot, and so, after a time, they move on; and, as they leave, we feel that the terms of their shared existence are so completely defined by brutality and lovelessness that it is no wonder that they do not wait, for, having lost their humanity, all hope in them is dead.

The day is now drawing to a close, and Estragon and Vladimir continue to wait for Godot to appear. But at last there comes a Boy to tell them that Godot will not come tonight but that he will surely come tomorrow. And when he asks what message he is to take back, Vladimir says: "Tell him . . . tell him you saw us." Then in a moment it is night, and Estragon asks: "Well, shall we go?" Vladimir says, "Yes, let's go." But, as the curtain falls, they do not move.

The second act of the play takes place on the following evening and on the same spot, though this time we find that a few leaves have begun to appear on the tree. Estragon and Vladimir resume their conversation of the night before, which moves along with the same aimless intensity, as they gather up into a shapeless heap the broken fragments of their lives. And whenever Estragon asks what they shall do, Vladimir's only answer is "Wait for Godot"; or when Estragon recalls his weariness and proposes that they leave, Vladimir simply says: "We can't. . . . We're waiting for Godot." After a time Pozzo and Lucky return: Pozzo now is blind; Lucky is dumb; and this is but the visible evidence, we feel, that confirms our earlier sense that they were utterly lost. They remain for a brief time and then move on, leaving Vladimir and Estragon beneath the tree to continue their vigil. Finally, as night falls, the Boy returns with another message from Godot, that he will not come today but that he is surely to be expected tomorrow. And when the Boy asks Vladimir if there is a message that he is in turn to take back to his master, Vladimir, after hesitating for a moment, replies: "Tell him . . . that you saw me." Then, after the Boy's departure, Vladimir asks, "Well? Shall we go?" And Estragon says, "Yes, let's go." But, again, as the curtain falls, they do not move.

Now these are the two acts of Beckett's play which are beautifully summarized in the lament that is uttered at one point by Estragon, when he says: "Nothing happens, nobody comes, nobody goes, it's awful!" This is precisely it: nothing does happen; two Chaplinesque hobos wait under a tree for someone called Godot, who never arrives; and, as they wait, they talk—like the dead talk—about their lives. Yet these two hobos are choreographic examples of ourselves, and, notwithstanding the unbroken stasis which Mr. Beckett maintains, he has managed here to produce a masterpiece of tragic drama no small part of whose power is, I suspect, a consequence of the acuteness with which it probes the dominant mood that grips our time.

And we shall misconstrue the fundamental meaning of the play if we take what Mr. Beckett has done to be a further contribution to the testimony of contemporary Existentialism. For the Existentialists have found a new gospel to preach—which is the gospel of the absurd; and it is "gospel" or "good news" for them because, in naming the source of our perplexities as the absurd, they have, if only in having found a name for it, gained access to a sense of transcension over it, at least to the extent of finding life bearable once again, upon the basis of a reinstatement of a kind of Stoic humanism. They have, in other words, ceased "waiting," and this is why, I think, Jean-Paul Sartre cannot therefore be regarded as a truly representative spokesman of our age. For the rest of us *are* "waiting," and *we* are the people to whom Mr. Eliot is speaking, when he tells us in "East Coker" to

> . . . wait without hope
> For hope would be hope for the wrong thing; wait without love
> For love would be love of the wrong thing; there is yet faith
> But the faith and the love and the hope are all in the waiting.[1]

Indeed, it may well be that in our time the religious attitude gains its most characteristic manifestation in a certain stylized suspicion of grandiosity in the intellectual and spiritual life. We yearn, of course, as much today as men have always yearned for the Truth that would be a joy and a gladness to the heart, but we no longer suppose that the way of the seeker is a way that involves disinterested speculation *about* this Truth, as though it were something quite outside ourselves and our history. Though we do not suppose that that Truth is identical with our subjectivity, we are convinced that that which is radically significant will be found within our human nature and our history. Yet the very labyrinthine complications of these, as they have been revealed by the modern sciences of human nature, preclude any easy satisfaction of our "ontological hunger." So, as Mr. Auden tells us, having now to submit ourselves to the discipline of "learning" the distance of God, we "wait," and, like the two hobos in Mr. Beckett's play, while we "wait" we talk to one another about our lives—which is our way of reaching after what is most really real by means of inwardness. We believe, as M. Gabriel Marcel says, that "to bear witness is to contribute to the growth or coming of that for which one testifies." [2] And we are certain that Rilke is right when he tells us:

Be patient towards all that is unsolved in your heart and try to love *the questions themselves* like locked rooms. . . . Do not now seek the answers, that cannot be given you because you would not be able to live them. And the point is, to live everything. *Live* the questions now. Perhaps you will then gradually, without noticing it, live along some distant day into the answer.[3]

We live, then, in a period in which the ultimate Meaning of our existence appears, in Heidegger's term, to be "withholding" itself. And in such a time it seems that what we can witness to with greatest assurance are those deep tendencies within our own nature which promise to lead us back again into proximity to the Truth. So our "waiting" assumes the form of inwardness and the disciplined cultivation of inwardness—and we talk to one another about our lives: it is not the latest cosmology that we are most deeply interested in, but, rather, it is the biography and the autobiography which promise us help in steering a course through "the vacuum of disintegration" and in addressing "the Void as 'Thou.' " [4]

This is the dominant mode of vision in the age of vigil in which we live, and it is a cultural and religious style that gains many expressions in the work of thinkers only tangentially related to the Christian community like the remarkable Frenchwoman, the late Simone Weil, or the German philosopher Martin Heidegger, and also in the work of many significant thinkers whose anchorage is most deeply in the Christian faith. One thinks, for example, of the French Catholic philosopher Marcel, of whom it is sometimes said by his less friendly critics that he is really more a psychologist than he is a philosopher, because he seems to be more deeply concerned with the human experience of metaphysical questions (the great questions of Being and God and the self) than with the questions themselves. It is argued that his principal concern appears to be more with the psychological exploration of man's experience of that which transcends him than with a genuinely metaphysical analysis of the mystery of existence; that he appears to be more concerned to make us feel what it is like to experience philosophic perplexity in an age of crisis than to furnish a metaphysical resolution of that perplexity. And these considerations are brought forward by his critics in order to intimate his lack of philosophic seriousness. But what these critics fail to recognize is precisely what it has been Marcel's major purpose to accomplish—namely, the establishment of the inescapability of metaphysics by means of the demonstration that man is by nature a creature of metaphysical passion. Marcel's way of doing this has involved an analysis of the respects in which the life of man is a life of dialogue, involving most essentially that "I-Thou" relation of which Martin Buber has spoken. And for Marcel the law of this relation is the law of fidelity: man is the being who can make pledges and herein lie his radical uniqueness and his glory. Indeed, "a code of ethics centered on fidelity," Marcel tells us, "is irresistibly led to become attached to what is more than human, to a desire for the unconditional which is the requirement and the very mark of the Absolute in us." [5] In other words, in a time of "waiting" we do not discover the ultimate meaning of our existence by way of building metaphysical systems that quickly move from that which is immediately known to that which is less evident and perhaps even utterly obscure. On the contrary: we begin to move toward the inner mystery of Being when we consent to be *present* to one another, to be available, to reveal ourselves to one another, for the recognition of the absolute "Thou" becomes possible only in the degree to which we have cultivated the discipline of responding to the particular presences into commerce with whom we are brought by the adventures of life. Marcel's metaphysic might, in fact, be said to be, at bottom, a metaphysic of presence that enjoins us to talk to one another about our lives.

And much the same sort of enjoinder might, I think, be regarded as implicit in the thought of a Protestant thinker like Rudolf Bultmann. The work of this remarkable theologian represents such enormous complication that any brief and informal characterization of it is likely to distort or to misrepresent the totality of his testimony. And yet I believe it would not be incorrect to say that, at bottom, Bultmann's writings during the last decade have been calculated to undermine the notion that the biblical kerygma is a system of objective truths about the universe. What he has contended is that the kerygma rests on those critical and decisive acts of God in Jesus Christ, that its truth is therefore the truth of a person, and that it is a truth that cannot be explicated except in terms of our relationship to that person. Faith is "the answer" to the kerygma—which is to say that the proper mode of our response to it is the decision to appropriate *for myself* the possibilities of redemption and creativity that it offers. This in turn involves a radical reorientation of the way in which I understand myself, self-prehension now proceeding in the light of the Cross and the Resurrection. And the theological enterprise does, in fact, for Bultmann involve nothing other than the systematic explication of the new self-understanding that is given in Christian faith: theology is, indeed, for him phenomenology of faith. What is said in the New Testament must be interpreted in terms of its significance for *my* existence, in terms of what it means *for me*. Now, of course, it is true that, if God has done something absolutely decisive for human existence in Jesus Christ, then it would seem that the question must be faced as to whether theological discourse must not itself therefore move finally toward a discussion not simply of Christian existence but also of its basis in the actual work of God. But this issue is not quite within the purview of my present concern, for I have brought forward the work of Rudolf Bultmann only for the sake of citing another example, this time in the Protestant theological community, of an enormously powerful and influential thinker who is defining the religious enterprise in our time in a way that, at bottom, really enjoins us to talk to one another about our lives, about what has happened to us. Here, in other words, as in many other contemporary Christian philosophers whose testimony might also be cited, we get a definition of what is religiously viable for our period in terms of the life of dialogue, in terms of communion with one another in love. It would seem, indeed, that much of the most advanced philosophic and religious intelligence of our day apprehends the spiritual universe in which modern man must live as being one very much like that inhabited by Samuel Beckett's Estragon and Vladimir.

Now what I have principally wanted to bring into view is the remarkable convergence of vision that appears when the currents of thought that I have been noticing are seen in relation to the kind of testimony that is taking shape in much of the finest imaginative literature of the present time. And here my best way of moving toward the kind of generalization that I want to make is to turn, first of all, to a novel by a young American writer which in recent years has been the cause of a most remarkable kind of spiritual reverberation amongst a continuously widening circle of readers: it is Mr. J. D. Salinger's *The Catcher in the Rye*.[6] The distinguished British critic, the late John Middleton Murry, remarked just a few months ago, shortly before his death, that this "is the only absolutely modern novel which has moved me deeply,"[7] but Murry was a man of an older generation, and much more significant, in a way, I think (because of what it tells us about the nature of the contemporary sensibility), is the confession that I have heard in the last four or five years from innumerable young people on college campuses and from many of my own students that nowhere else in contemporary literature do they find their sense of the world and of themselves more sensitively rendered than in this book.

The protagonist of Mr. Salinger's novel is sixteen-year-old Holden Caulfield, who, knowing that he is to be dropped for poor grades by his fashionable prep school in Pennsylvania, suddenly decides, just a day or so before dismissal for Christmas, to leave the campus early and not to report home until he is expected. So he escapes to New York City, where he spends two days; and the novel consists of the story that he tells us in his own words of what his life has been like and of what he saw and experienced during those two days—at the end of which he finally turns up at his parents' New York apartment. And when his ten-year-old sister Phoebe asks him to explain his failure at school (which is only one of many from which he has been expelled), he says:

"Oh, God, Phoebe, don't ask me. I'm sick of everybody asking me that. A million reasons why. It was one of the worst schools I ever went to. It was full of phonies. And mean guys. You never saw so many mean guys in your life. For instance, if you were having a bull session in somebody's room, and somebody wanted to come in, nobody'd let them in if they were some dopey, pimply guy. Everybody was always *locking* their door when somebody wanted to come in. . . . Just because he was boring and pimply. I don't even feel like talking about it. It was a stinking school. Take my word. . . . Even the couple of *nice* teachers on the faculty, they were phonies, too. There was this one old guy, Mr. Spencer. His wife was always giving you hot chocolate and all that stuff, and they were really pretty nice. But you should've seen him when the headmaster, old Thurmer, came in the history class and sat down in the back of the room . . . he'd start interrupting what old Spencer was saying to crack a lot of corny jokes. Old Spencer'd practically kill himself chuckling and smiling and all, like as if Thurmer was a goddam prince or something. . . . It would've made you puke, I swear it would. . . . God, Phoebe! I can't explain. I just didn't like anything that was *hap*pening at Pencey. I can't explain."

After patiently listening to a lengthy recital of this sort, little Phoebe finally says to Holden: "You don't like *any*thing that's happening." And Holden is very quickly unsettled by her trenchancy: he insists that she is wrong and that there are some things that he likes, but the piqued tone of his denial betrays that her dart has painfully struck home. And, indeed, she has, in a way, spoken truly, for Holden is at odds with the world, and, like the true romantic, his melancholy is a consequence of the gross disparity that he everywhere discovers between life and the dream.

That which Holden is most dismayed by in life is what his colloquialism habituates him to call "phoniness": it is the general emotional atrophy and insensibility in people that he rages against, for it leads them to say one thing when they mean another. And, what is even more distressing for him, it leads them to be unavailable, not to be present, for human beings can encounter one another only when they are honest and willing to run the risks of speaking the truth. But nowhere can Holden find such integrity, and it is his fierce consciousness of its absence that constitutes the real dramatic center of the book. His mind is, like Huck Finn's, a mind that is fully "awake" to the casual *bad faith* by which human relations are so generally corrupted, and, like Huck, his own frequent lies represent his way of defending himself against conventional dishonesty.

Now Holden's way of searching for truth and love is to listen attentively to what men say, and his consciousness of their moral vacuousness is conveyed to us in his consciousness of how empty the noises are that we conventionally make in our daily communications with one another. Here are some examples of what I mean. Just before leaving Pencey Prep, he pays a visit one afternoon to old Mr. and Mrs. Spencer. Mr. Spencer is recovering from an attack of grippe, but, even so, he energetically dresses Holden down for having flunked out of school. And in the course of the conversation he remarks: "I had the privilege of meeting your mother and dad when they had their little chat with Dr. Thurmer some weeks ago. They're grand people." Which causes Holden to think to himself, "Grand. There's a word I really hate. It's a phony. I could puke every time I hear it." As the afternoon wears on, Mrs. Spencer offers Holden a cup of hot chocolate, but he refuses it, wanting now to get out and be gone. And he tells us that, as he shut their door behind him, he thought he heard Mr. Spencer yell "Good luck!" at him. But, says Holden, "I hope not. I hope to hell not. I'd never yell 'Good luck!' at anybody. It sounds terrible, when you think about it." And on many other occasions he is set on edge by the people who tell him that he's "marvelous" or "swell" or who, in bidding him farewell after having met him for a first time, say, "Glad to've met you." At these times Holden feels "depressed and lousy": "It just kills me," he says. And what he is set on edge by is the insincerity, the evasiveness, and the bad faith that are revealed in our common speech.

For at the bottom of the intensity and the wild erraticism of this boy are a profound sadness and embarrassment over the ugly slum of the spirit that the world appears to be. He is a boy who is biased by the need for love, but what he generally finds in people is the slothful moral imagination, the undeveloped heart, an incapacity for generousness, an unwillingness to be genuinely present to one another. And there seems to be no escape from his basic human solitude.

This is why he bears his little dead brother Allie constantly in mind, and this is why he is so deeply sustained by his sister Phoebe. For Allie, he says, "never got mad at anybody." And of his sister he says: "You'd like her. I mean if you tell old Phoebe something, she knows exactly what the hell you're talking about." So from her he hides nothing, and when she finally asks him what it is that he really wants to be, he suddenly recalls having recently followed a little boy down a street as the child quietly sang to himself "If a body catch a body coming through the rye"; and he tells Phoebe that he thinks he would like to be "the catcher in the rye." And what, I think, he means is precisely what he says: he wants to break out of his loneliness; he wants to be able to reach across the gulfs that separate us from one another and to catch people before they run off into their little shells. And he wants this because he wants others besides Phoebe to whom he can talk about his life; he wants others with whom there need be no reservations, before whom he can be vulnerable, and to whom he can be really present. Which is to say, again, that Holden's universe is the universe of Estragon and Vladimir, for he too is waiting for a great disclosure and for a brave new world, and while he waits he wants to find those to whom he can say what he needs to say.

Here, then, is what it is that gives to this book its exemplary character and that makes it speak so profoundly to the young men and women of the present time, for the story of Holden Caulfield lines itself up behind the feeling that we are all, in various ways, today committed to, that perhaps the best way of surviving this present time is for us to become "catchers in the rye," to seek self-definition in and through the most primitive realities of our human togetherness, and to talk to one another about our lives. This is, at any rate, what I discover the most sensitive young people whom I meet to be regarding as the way to live through the present interim, through this "age between the ages." And this compass by which the young are steering their lives is not only recommended by many great strategists of contemporary thought in the realm of philosophy and theology but, as I am now suggesting Mr.

Salinger's novel indicates, this is also the anchorage to which the poetic vision of our day would have us turn.

Mr. Malcolm Cowley, in commenting on the way in which the human experience is organized by many of our finest younger artists who have entered the literary life in the last ten or fifteen years, has spoken of the "personalism" in the new literature.[8] And his term is, I think, well chosen, for when one thinks of such representative books of the last several years as Carson McCullers' *The Member of the Wedding,* Jean Stafford's *The Catherine Wheel,* Elizabeth Hardwick's *The Ghostly Lover,* Robie Macaulay's *The Disguises of Love,* Ralph Ellison's *The Invisible Man,* and Mr. Salinger's *The Catcher in the Rye*—when one thinks of such books as these, it does, indeed, appear that much of the best contemporary literature is biased toward a kind of "personalism" and that many of our writers are wanting to tell us that the particular quarry from which we are to derive the deepest insights into the meaning of human existence is the realm of dialogue, the realm of personal experience.

It is, in fact, this stress of the vision lying behind much recent poetry and fiction and even drama that defines the shape of the contemporary imagination and that sets it apart so sharply from the quality of imagination that lay behind much of the *avant-garde* literature of twenty and thirty years ago. For when one thinks at random of such modern classics as Ezra Pound's *Hugh Selwyn Mauberley,* Eliot's *The Waste Land,* Hemingway's *The Sun Also Rises,* and Malraux's *Man's Fate,* one is reminded that, despite their great variousness, their underlying intention is to produce an evaluation of the disordered world of modern life. Nor is the voice that lies behind these books given to speaking in muted tones: it is an upraised voice that intends to alter the course of history. But just as the metaphysical vision of our time has very often tended to move from detached speculation about the objective universe toward the kind of personalism that I have indicated, so too has there been an analogous movement in the poetic vision of the period, for the position of the authors of *The Cocktail Party* or *The Confidential Clerk* and *The Old Man and the Sea* is obviously very different from what it was thirty or thirty-five years ago. And the nature of the reversal that has been accomplished here is most fully revealed in the work of those younger writers whose testimony I have been adducing.

This was not, of course, the development in the literary life that we expected after the close of World War II. We were then prepared, it is true, to record the emergence of a new phase in the history of the modern imagination, and we assumed that, whatever it was, it must surely be new, since—we told ourselves—every postwar literature expresses the disenchantment, the defeatism, the despair, the sense of nullity, or whatever else it is that constitutes the predominant mood in the time that follows the time of anarchy and turbulence. What we had most immediately in mind was the trend that poetry and fiction had followed in the twenties and thirties, when our major writers had undertaken, as if by an act of general consent, to evaluate the world to which they returned from Belleau Wood, from Saint-Mihiel and the Argonne Forest—a world in which theirs appeared to be a generation utterly lost and without grounds for faith or anticipation. We had in mind the blighted hopes and the sad disillusionments of those young men who wrote books like *The Enormous Room, Three Soldiers,* and *In Our Time;* we had in mind the sullen, angry intensity that produced, in the thirties, books like the *Studs Lonigan* trilogy and *The Grapes of Wrath*. And, recalling this earlier time, we expected, after 1945, that the youngest generation of poets and novelists, on returning home from military service in the second major war of this century, would also produce a literature that, in its special way, would mirror and evaluate the landscape of the contemporary period.

So—let us say, shortly after Hiroshima—we began to remind ourselves that we must keep alert and prepared to notice and celebrate "the new fiction" and "the new poetry" on the day they should arrive. And we were certain that they were expectable momentarily. The oppressive burden of our historical awareness compelled preoccupation with the ravelment and incoherence of contemporary life: we knew what the issues were—pervasive bad faith abroad and the subversion of individual freedom at home by the adoption of a whole new set of tactics for guaranteeing internal security, by both of which Western democracy seemed to be desperately threatened. Here lay, we felt, the real crisis of our time, and we eagerly awaited the counterpoise to fear and trembling that the new postwar literature would provide—for how, we wondered, could it possibly evade the troubles of our generation? We were—that is, American literary intellectuals as a class—a little wary of the Paris Existentialists and their doctrinaire crusades in the realm of ideas; but, however much skepticism we might profess with respect to Jean-Paul Sartre's concept of *la littérature engagée,* it was, nevertheless, something of the sort that we wanted and expected —and that we did not receive.

Indeed, a great deal of the activity of the journalists who write for the literary columns of the liberal weeklies and the literary supplements of the Sunday press has been expended recently in an effort to comprehend the fact that our postwar literature has not, on the whole, been "engaged" with the crises and distempers of contemporary history, as we had expected it would be. Dramatists like Tennessee Williams and Jane Bowles and Robert Anderson and novelists like Peter Taylor and William Goyen and Jean Stafford and Frederick Buechner have seemed to be resisting the demands of the public life for attention today and have dwelt upon the relationships and the dilemmas of the private life, the psychological penalties exacted by loneliness and the need for love. The theme of childhood, for example, recurs again and again in the recent literature of the novel, in Jean Stafford's *The Mountain Lion,* in Truman Capote's *Other Voices, Other Rooms,* in Carson McCullers' *The Member of the Wedding,* and in many other books by their contemporaries. The reason for this doubtless lies in part in our modern awareness of the psychologically crucial importance of infancy and childhood; but, more fundamentally, it has to be explained (as the English critic Mr. Henry Reed has suggested, in commenting upon similar thematic patterns in recent British literature) by the fact that

In a world of darkness we learn to hug that memory of comparative light. A child may be unhappy, but it is never wholly so; its happiness is not the mere absence of pain, and it has an innocence which the happiness of adult life is too complex to have. It is natural to turn and attempt to recapture and understand and detail that lost possibility of Eden.[9]

And—in addition to the novels of childhood and adolescent reverie—the difficult marriage, the intricate maze of personal relationships within a family, the ambiguous sexual identity with all of its hazardous involvements, the crisis of self-recognition in middle age, and many other similar themes are to be found in the novels of the present period. Our best young writers today are, it seems, attempting to embrace the permanent truths of man's condition in the context of the fundamental human relationships. And, in the process of this undertaking, they are fashioning a style of their own which suggests that they no longer live under the dispensation of Hemingway but rather live now under the dispensation of the magisterial figure of Henry James. The new prose is very far indeed from the terse, tight-lipped telegraphy of Hemingway which was for so long the normative speech for the writer of our time, though it by no means represents a reaction toward a new baroque extravagance of diction. It springs rather from a renewed delight in the vivacious and brilliant processes through which the intellect asserts itself in imaginative literature, and it is characterized by the kind of richly personal complexity of style that is perhaps the common signature shared by such otherwise different writers as Peter Taylor and William Styron, Elizabeth Hardwick and Jean Stafford, George Lanning and Frederick Buechner.

As one reflects, then, upon the literary situation of our period, one is led, more and more, to feel that such books as André Malraux's *Man's Fate* and Ignazio Silone's *Bread and Wine* are not likely to be written in the next few years by the younger practitioners of the art who are active on the contemporary scene. That there should be no expectation of an insurgence at the present time of such a literature may at first appear to be strange. For, as Professor Lionel Trilling remarked a few years ago, "our fate, for better or worse, is political," and we are "in the full tide of those desperate perceptions . . . which . . . haunt and control our minds with visions of losses worse than that of existence— losses of civilization, personality, humanness" [10] and of the most fundamental decencies in our common life. And so it might be supposed that our poets and novelists could no more resist the demands of the public life for attention today than could poets in the thirties like Stephen Spender and W. H. Auden in England, or novelists like Malraux and Silone on the Continent and John Dos Passos in America. The fact is, however, that one looks in vain today for a young writer on the American scene struggling to contain within the terms of significant artistic statement the moral and psychological drama of, let us say, an Alger Hiss or the late Senator Joseph McCarthy.

It is often argued by the Sunday book reviewers that the failure of our younger writers to grapple head-on with the great public crises of our time is simply to be explained in terms of their craven timorousness before the difficulties that the age presents: theirs, we are told, is "the silent generation," "the careful generation." But this is, I believe, to take a far too simple view of what they are determined by. For their plight consists, fundamentally, in their situation, in their residence within what Marcel calls a "broken world." They are overcome, as most of us are, with "a general dismay at the results of five centuries of progress and widening enlightenment." [11] It is not that they have turned away from contemporary life but rather that the uneasy truce of the cold war that separates East from West, the shrinkage of personal liberty throughout the world, the pervasive bad faith, the hell of global insecurity in which we live, point for them not simply to a breakdown in the machinery of modern society but to something in the nature of man which cannot be grasped by the mathematically precise assignations of guilt and innocence characteristic of orthodox leftist liberal thought. As Mr. Auden remarked in his "New Year Letter" of 1940:

> The situation of our time
> Surrounds us like a baffling crime.

And all of our equipment for the detection and containment of the malevolent forces only

> Extends the area of the crime
> Until the guilt is everywhere,
> And more and more we are aware,
> However miserable may be
> Our parish of immediacy,
> How small it is, how, far beyond,
> Ubiquitous within the bond
> Of one impoverishing sky,
> Vast spiritual disorders lie.[12]

Our situation today is so different from that of the nineteen-thirties: for the author of *In Dubious Battle* and *The Grapes of Wrath* and his generation "there remained the illusion that history could *still be altered*—altered by the outraged individual voice of the observer." [13] But we are given some measure of the extent to which in the intervening years this illusion has been shattered in, for example, the case of Mr. Richard Wright, who, as a Negro writer, is surely in possession of an urgent social subject. In his novel of 1940, *Native Son,* Mr. Wright gave us, if not an altogether artistically coherent, certainly a most deeply felt and moving statement of the tragic deprivations that have been the burden of the American Negro. And it was a novel whose violent rhetoric was the exacerbated outcry of a man who had looked with painful steadiness at a segment of social reality. But his more recent book, *The Outsider,* though clearly the product of a writer who has a genius for the novel, is marred by a certain insecurity of tone, a certain strident petulance, that was not so markedly present in the earlier novel and that suggests that the metaphysical hysteria which all of us experience intermittently today has also overtaken Mr. Wright. He no longer talks straightforwardly about contemporary social reality with the confidence and certainty of his former manner, but, rather, presents us with what is almost a Kafkaesque *grotesquerie* which, though hedged about with all sorts of sophistications that appeal to the cultivated reader, clearly reveals the writer's uneasiness today before the social fact of which, in an earlier time, he was more fully in possession.

I have been led to invoke the name of Franz Kafka, partly no doubt by a kind of reflex, for at this middle point in the progress of twentieth-century literature one does not talk for long about the lay of the land without mentioning his name. The claustral, nightmare world of his novels is the world in which we very often feel ourselves to be living, and it is the world in terms of which much of the testimony about the human condition in recent literature has to be understood. In *The Trial,* for example, the hero Joseph K. is accused one morning of a crime he did not commit and the nature of which he cannot even discover. He seeks a court hearing, enters into transactions with a dubious attorney, tries to find allies, and desperately attempts to reach the higher authorities who dispense the court's justice. But he never succeeds. And, at the end, on the evening before his thirty-first birthday, two officials of the court escort him from his house to an old quarry on the outskirts of the city where they stab him to death. Here is a world in which the defenseless individual is at every point haunted and harassed and pushed about by recondite powers whose pursuit of him is so relentless and unremitting that in the end he begins to confuse his real identity with that which he has somewhere been given in an official dossier, the exact contents of which remain forever undiscoverable.

The general bureaucratization of modern life is a phenomenon which provides one of the themes that runs throughout Kafka's entire work. In story after story and in novel after novel man is caught within unwieldy mechanisms whose operations are gallingly dilatory and fortuitous. "In fact," says Mr. Max Lerner, "by a wild irony, in this regime of order and law it is accident that is decisive. Despite the oppressive anxiety of Kafka's protagonist to fulfill his quest and come to terms with his universe, despite his desperate straining to make even the slightest headway, he is hopelessly entangled in a network of casual incidents. The most irrelevant act may lead to the widest consequence; the trivial is canonized." [14] The whole sequence of events in *The Trial* or *The Castle,* we say, is improbable. But then, on taking thought, we realize that Kafka thrusts us into the very center of the maelstrom of contemporary life as it is daily reported upon in the great newspapers of the world.

Indeed, the profound influence that Kafka has exerted upon many writers—poets and novelists and dramatists—in recent years is, I think, due to a renewal among them of a sense (which they are aware of sharing with him) of "the transcendent, of an absolute indicated by, but not contained in, the experience of this ambiguous world." [15] So that poets today like John Berryman and Randall Jarrell and novelists like John Hawkes and Robert Penn Warren, as they talk about our world, often seem at the same time to be mindful of something like Karl Barth's *totaliter aliter* (the "Wholly Other"), even when there is not the slightest religious reference of any explicit sort in their work. They have, like Kafka, gone "beyond the problem of man facing his society to the problem of man facing himself and the unknown and inaccessible within him." [16] And in the vacuum of contemporary life they are often at the point, we feel, of addressing the Void as "Thou."

They—most of them—do not yet, of course, really know how to do this, and so they dwell upon the "I-Thou" relation not in its extra-mundane but rather in its intramundane aspect. In a world in which, as Marcel says, "the preposition 'with' . . . seems more and more to be losing its meaning," [17] they insist ever more determinedly upon the preciousness of personal relations. Indeed, it may well be that the refusal of our younger novelists to write the kind of straightforward novel of society or politics that was being written in the nineteen-thirties is not, as it is sometimes argued, a timorous evasion of today's public realities, but stems rather from a desire to celebrate and safeguard the personal life, since they believe it to be threatened by the collective *as such*. In any event, our young poets often address their poems to their wives and intimate friends, and our young novelists choose to write of the crises and dilemmas of the private life. William Styron (*Lie Down in Darkness*) has written of the moral dilemmas of a family whose members cannot love and who are therefore doomed people. Jean Stafford (*The Catherine Wheel*) has written of an exquisite woman, Katherine Congreve, in early middle age, living alone in a great house in New England and gradually discovering the sterility of her beautifully ordered life which does not really flow out into any other life, in love and responsibility. George Lanning (*This Happy Rural Seat*) has brilliantly written of a man, Herbert Komar, who (like the hero of Henry James's *The Beast in the Jungle*), discovering at the age of sixty the emptiness of the uninvolved, unentangled life that for years he has led—eating in drab restaurants and living in dismal rooming houses—seeks to rectify it, "too late . . . but not *too* late." And Elizabeth Pollet (*Family Romance*) writes of hazardous emotional ambivalences in the relation between a father and daughter. And Mr. Malcolm Cowley says that they and their contemporaries have created "a tidy room in Bedlam."[18] But the unity of the testimony about contemporary life that is implicit in their work is, I believe, more sensitively formulated by Mr. Robert Gorham Davis in the following concise summary:

. . . the fiction of this period is as unified in its attitudes and dominant concerns as the fiction of the 'twenties and 'thirties. The three periods are, moreover, very directly related. The impulse of the 'twenties was toward an anarchic individualism which turned out to be inadequate in the social crises of the 'thirties. A good many writers and intellectuals then swung to the other extreme and surrendered their individual moral consciences to reformist programs of a more or less totalitarian nature. . . . But after 1939 there was an increasingly strong reaction against totally political solutions.

Now the novelists are starting all over again and saying that simple human affection and honesty about oneself are all that can be counted on.[19]

Now, of course, it is by no means improper that this whole tendency in recent literature should be made to bear the brunt of some critical pressure and that we should ask whether or not the reversal that it represents has entailed any loss. And no sooner is this question raised than we are put in mind of what is either a present weakness or one that is sometimes dangerously skirted in the new literature. For the desire to portray the human reality in dialogical terms, in terms of personal communion, may and sometimes does result in a tendency to render human life as if it were (in Langmead Casserley's striking metaphor) merely "a chaos of mutually irrelevant duets"[20] that are quite separable from any historical context. Indeed, it is just here that the kind of sensibility expressed, say, in *The Catcher in the Rye* differs most radically from that which governs many of those books which we regard as exemplifying the great classic modern style. For, as Mr. Trilling has observed, that which distinguishes the writers who formed that style is that they all "in one way or another turned their passions, their adverse, critical, and very intense passions, upon the condition of the polity."[21] Books like Joyce's *Ulysses* and Mann's *The Magic Mountain*, Elias Canetti's *Auto da Fé* and Silone's *Bread and Wine*, are so memorable, partly because of their deep saturation in the historical consciousness. They portray human individuals as living under the pressures of a tragic confluence of historical circumstances, and the focus is upon the public world of Dublin, of Vienna, of Fascist Italy, and so on. It is true that the focus is also upon the inner complexity of the individual life, but this is shown "precisely at the point where it overlaps the general social and political interest." [22] What we are given is a sense of contemporaneity—a sense, as Mr. Eliot says, that "History is now . . ." In such modern texts as Pound's *Cantos,* Eliot's *The Waste Land,* and Hermann Broch's *The Sleepwalkers* we feel that the age is conscious of itself and in terms of some vast metaphor about itself is embracing a philosophy of history. But, on the other hand, engaging as it is, we yet feel something closeted and hermetic about the world of Holden Caulfield or of Carson McCullers' Frankie Addams (*The Member of the Wedding*), and, indeed, in much of the literature of the new "personalism," it is the very idea of history that seems to be resisted—and the *tendency* is to present human life as though it were "a chaos of mutually irrelevant duets" rather than "a vast chorale . . . [which must always be] inefficiently and discordantly rendered." [23]

We have here, however, what is only a particular illustration of a general dilemma facing those whose dispensation it is to live in this present time of waiting, of vigil. We feel, on the one hand, that ours must be a kind of holding operation, that we must shore up our lives against disaster by huddling together about the human campfire, and that in this way (in Marcel's words) we may "become attached to what is more than human" and discover in one another "the requirement and the very mark of the Absolute." And yet, on the other hand, it seems that, if we ignore the rough weathers of history, the campfire may be snuffed out and the world of the "interim" may become a wilderness and a desert. So our problem, then, appears to be one of learning how to be patient and how to "wait," without at the same time consenting to a virtual abdication from the historical scene. And it is to be hoped that in the years to come the genius of men like Marcel and Bultmann (and Buber and Niebuhr and Tillich), and of men like Beckett and Salinger, will more and more engage itself with this question, for it precipitates us into our deepest quandary, wherein much help is needed that they have not yet given us.

VI

Beneath the Hammer of Truth

WE GIVE A kind of attention today to the major literature of our period that we give to no other department of our cultural life. Our philosophy —and especially that which is in the custodianship of the academicians —has long since ceased to "make news" and has become merely a kind of esoteric and highly complicated calculus that has little relevance at all to the elementary facts of human existence. The social sciences, though they profess to deal with the ancient existential questions, very often do so by way of attempting to gloss over the intractable ambiguities of the human story with some sort of simplistic statistical equation; and, too frequently, the language of the social scientist, with its cumbrous jargon, has the effect of overinflating what is essentially banal and platitudinous. The Continental Existentialists have, to be sure, brought a new excitement into philosophic discussion; and, occasionally, there comes along a rare sociologist like David Riesman or C. Wright Mills who has a fresh and significant report to make upon the condition of man in our time. But, in both areas, the unorthodoxy of the *avant-garde* prevents it from having the kind of impact upon these disciplines that would restore to them an air of urgency and importance; and thus they do not command the kind of attention from the general educated public that they once did. Indeed, on the contrary, I think we feel, if any illumination at all is to be had of our secret nightmares and the deepest issues of our perplexity, that it is likely to be gotten not from our philosophers or social scientists but from a few prophetic spirits in the theological community and from the major poets and novelists of our day. Here, in the books of Lawrence and Kafka and Mann and Faulkner, of Rilke and Yeats and Dylan Thomas

—here, we think, is a kind of modern revelation that helps us to accept the ache that is within us and that has been aroused by the necessity of living amidst the dilapidation of our time. As we enter the universe that these writers inhabit, we may be led to cry out with Marlowe's Mephistopheles: "Why this is hell"—though we shall doubtless also be led to add, as he did, "nor am I out of it!" And if no exit out of our Inferno is described, at least we may be drawn more deeply into it—which is perhaps, after all, the right way, since, as Mr. Eliot tells us in the *Quartets,* we must "Descend lower . . ." before attempting to scale the bright Mount of Purgation.

Nor does the Christian intelligentsia present any longer the kind of exception that it once did to the general receptivity to the great literature of our period, though its transactions with the modern literary arts do still occasionally reflect a somewhat too inflexible resolution to use them for its own special purposes and to cast them aside with a gesture of impatience when they resist such plunderage. In a recent encounter, for example, with a group of clergymen before whom I had been discussing contemporary movements in poetry and the novel, I found one gentleman whose remarks did not suggest that he had had any direct dealings of his own with recent literature but which did indicate that he had somewhere overheard the rumor that T. S. Eliot and W. H. Auden are "Christian" poets. So he was quite prepared to acknowledge that these men might possibly have important things to say to us, but, having also overheard somewhere else the rumor that William Faulkner is a dangerously decadent artificer in obscenity and violence, he was unyielding in his insistence that Mr. Faulkner's work should be denounced as a corrupting force in our cultural life today. He concluded his remarks with the rather crudely phrased question: "Why is it that these modern writers must always wallow around in so much filth?" And he was quite blunt in his refusal to lend an attentive ear to my representation of Faulkner's work as revealing a moral imagination controlled by a body of assumptions that are a detrital residue of a Protestantism that was once the formative factor in the regional culture out of which he comes.

Now it is, I fear, such an attitude that often controls the Protestant intelligence in its dealings with the modern arts. It is an attitude that is characterized by a great eagerness to pre-empt the work of those artists who are themselves prepared unambiguously to give their suffrage to a recognizably orthodox version of the Christian faith; and it is an attitude that is also characterized by an unwillingness to enter into a reciprocal relationship with the work of those artists who represent complications of belief that do not, on first examination, appear to be easily assimilable to a Christian vision of things. This is, of course, a kind of inflexibility that is untrue to the genius of what Professor Tillich has called "the Protestant principle," [1] and it must always be a disabling embarrassment to Protestantism, as it seeks to relate itself to the frontiers of thought and expression in contemporary culture.

It was something of this sort that not long ago I sensed as lying behind the conception of a certain project in literary discussion, being launched under religious auspices, in which I had been invited to participate. And I expressed my misgivings about it in a letter to a friend who, as a brilliant younger figure in American philosophy and a member of the Yale department, had also been invited to join in the undertaking. This is a part of what he said in reply, and his response provides me with a kind of text upon which to base this present lesson:

I could not be more in agreement with you. . . . What I would reject are those who simply want to use one of the cultural channels—art, literature, etc.—in what Tillich would call a heteronomous way, simply as another mouthpiece for expressing the new faith—i.e., the new paradoxical extravaganza just imported from abroad. Cultural mediation is a difficult and, it may be even, tragic business, in the sense that one has to take the medium seriously and grant it a limited autonomy—which means that it has an effect on what you are trying to say: the cultural channels, in other words, are not simply transparent props or tools or loud-speakers with which to amplify the voice. Perhaps the test of a man's genuine interest in this regard is to ask him whether he recognizes this relative autonomy and whether he is willing to accept all the consequences it may entail.

Now this is an excellent statement of what is, I think, an essentially true position, and at this point it comes pat to my purpose, since it enables me to commemorate the fact that it is precisely upon the autonomy of the art that the major theorists of poetry in our time have insisted.[2] And in this connection what has been their general testimony is very neatly summed up by Mr. Allen Tate, when he remarks in the Preface of his book *On the Limits of Poetry,* in commenting upon his title with its echo of Lessing, that in the essays that are here collected he finds himself to be

talking most of the time about what poetry cannot be expected to do to save mankind from the disasters in which poetry itself must be involved: that, I suppose, is a "limit" of poetry. Lessing says that poetry is not painting or sculpture; I am saying in this book, with very little systematic argument, that it is neither religion nor social engineering.[3]

Neither religion nor social engineering . . . nor philosophy, nor science, nor politics, but, as Mr. T. S. Eliot has said, simply "excellent words in excellent arrangement":[4] this is what poetry is. Which means, I take it, that the language of imaginative literature does not lead us beyond itself into some external realm of meaning; it is, rather, a language that is so thoroughly composed and that is so heavily charged with imaginative intensity that, unlike other forms of discourse, it is capable of capturing attention *intransitively* upon itself.[5] It is, indeed, the one form of discourse that, in its operations, manages to avoid any bifurcation between the thing or event and the words which refer to it. The language of poetry does not convey any rhetorical propositions about the issues of religion or politics or psychology or science; that is to say, it does not conduct the mind beyond itself to anything at all but rather leads us deeper and deeper into itself, in a process of exploration. And the "import" of poetry, as Mrs. Langer has said, "is not the literal assertion made in the words, but the way the assertion is made and this involves the sound, the tempo, the aura of associations of the words, long or short sequences of ideas, the wealth or poverty of transient imagery that contains them, the sudden arrest of fantasy by pure fact, or of familiar fact by sudden fantasy, the suspense of literal meaning by a sustained ambiguity resolved in a long-awaited key word, and the unifying, all-embracing artifice of rhythm."[6] The values of poetic art, in other words, are terminal values, and poetry does not "say" anything about anything at all. If, in short, you look for doctrine in it, you will have misconceived its true nature, for the poet is not a philosopher or a theologian but rather an artist who contrives, in Coleridge's phrase, a "species of composition"—and the word "composition" is here to be taken in its literal meaning of something shaped or fashioned, in this case a patterned mosaic in language.

But it is of the nature of a "composition" to *organize* something— and surely, someone will rejoin, poetry organizes something other than, say, merely the idea of poetry itself, and indeed it does. And Coleridge tells us in the famous fourteenth chapter of the *Biographia* what is here involved, when he speaks of the poet's fundamental problem as being that of "the balance or reconciliation of opposite or discordant qualities."[7] Now one reckless way of interpreting this oft-invoked formula—and the history of its exegesis furnishes many examples of recklessness—is to regard the "discordant qualities" which the poet strives to reconcile as growing out of that particular tension between order and disorder which is central to the poetic process. That is to say, the poet, when he sits down to write his poem or his novel, is in the situation of being one who has attained an expert skill in the supervision of words and who therefore possesses, whatever else he lacks, an *ordered* language—within which, now, he seeks to contain the *disorder* of experience and to do so in such a way as to create an "impractical stasis" that commands an act of "intransitive attention." [8] And every successful work of literary art might be regarded as being the result of the poet's conciliation of these discordancies.

But perhaps we are closer to Coleridge's actual implication if we regard the poet's conciliatory function as being exercised simply with respect to the discordancies within experience itself. This conciliatory function, however, as it has been displayed in the greatest literature in the tradition, has not involved—if I may paraphrase a famous line of Samuel Johnson's—any yoking together by violence of heterogeneous ideas, for this is not the way of the poet but, as we vulgarly say, of the "theoretician." [9] The poet's way has, rather, involved such a dramatization of the discordancies of life as renders them seizable by the imagination: "thesis" and "antithesis" have not been contained within some false and superficial "synthesis," but rather they have been rendered in all the ragged unevenness of their contradiction. The experiential urgency of the antinomy has, in a way, been "frozen," "as permanently as a logical formula, but without, like the formula, leaving all but the logic out" [10]—so that it has been made capable of captivating "the contemplative eye of the mind." [11] That is to say, the poet is distinguished not so much by his skill in producing rhetorical explanations of the "opposite or discordant qualities" in experience as he is by his skill in rendering these qualities, in dramatizing them, in making them concrete before the gaze of the mind. Or, as a final way of putting it, we may say that in his "compositions" he organizes the common human experience: he gives us a version of our human situation, but he gives us no propositions about it; he simply makes us look at it, and the meaning of what we look at appears to be quite indistinct from the form in which it is presented to us—so much so, indeed, that, in describing the mode of poetry's existence, we feel compelled to use such language as my friend used in his letter to me and to speak of its "autonomy."

When we characterize poetic art, then, as autonomous, we are say-ing, as Mr. Archibald MacLeish has remarked in a recent essay, that "Poetry is not interpretation," [12] or, as he put it some years ago in the famous tag from "Ars Poetica" which I quoted in an earlier chapter:

> A poem should not mean
> But be.

But this is not at all to say that the high forms of imaginative literature do not speak of the common human experience, for they do—but they do so not by way of generalizing upon it but rather by way of forcing us deeper and deeper into it. They impose an order upon it, but it is an order "which leaves it still the chaos and confusion which it really is. . . . In poetry—in the greatest poetry—experience *as it is* may be possessed." [13]

Now this characteristic of art (and it is true not only of literature but also of music and painting) must, I suspect, have figured in the thinking of Kierkegaard when he stressed, as he often does in his writ-ings, the profound difference between the aesthetic mind and the religious mind. For the aesthetic mind is, in Kierkegaard's concept of it, primarily characterized by an openness to experience and by the lack of any impulse to judge the experiences which the human adven-ture brings our way. And this is why, he would say, it lacks the *seriousness* of the ethical mind and the religious mind, for, though receptive to all experiences, it does not, in the name of a particular ex-perience, make any attack upon reality. It refuses to "get out of the poetical and into the existential"; it finds the human drama enor-mously interesting, but it is not led by its contemplation of it to make any decisive choices or to embrace any radical imperatives. This is Kierkegaard's conception of the aesthetic mind and of the great remove at which it lives from the existential realm, which is the realm of religion. And it is a conception which is adumbrated in these lines from Mr. Auden's "New Year Letter," in which he says:

> Art in intention is mimesis
> But, realised, the resemblance ceases;
> Art is not life and cannot be
> A midwife to society.
> For art is a *fait accompli*.
> What they should do, or how or when
> Life-order comes to living men
> It cannot say, for it presents

Already lived experience
Through a convention that creates
Autonomous completed states.
Though their particulars are those
That each particular artist knows,
Unique events that once took place
Within a unique time and space,
In the new field they occupy,
The unique serves to typify,
Becomes, though still particular,
An algebraic formula,
An abstract model of events
Derived from dead experiments,
And each life must itself decide
To what and how it be applied.[14]

Here, then, we have immediately before us the great and profound difference between the poetic orientation to reality and the religious. The former, it appears, leads to a desire to face experience, in all its concrete richness and plenitude, whereas the latter prompts us to make decisions as to how and where we should "apply" or adjust ourselves to the problematic circumstances of life.

So we confront the question now as to whether or not the aesthetic mind has any really fundamental significance for the religious mind. And it is a question the answer to which immediately begins to become apparent when we regard the chief faculty of the aesthetic mind as being the imagination and the chief faculty of the religious mind as being the will, for surely we ought to have no difficulty at all in seeing that the will cannot be effective unless it has a clear and lucid awareness of the situation in relation to which it must act and that it is not within its capacity to provide itself with this awareness. Indeed, it is just here that we may perceive the great and indispensable service which the imagination may perform for the religious life, for, by virtue of the heightened awareness of life that it affords, "it saves the energy of the will from wastage" [15] and therefore makes possible a religious response to life that is relevant to the actual facts of human experience.

Here we have, it seems to me, what must always be the most compelling reason for the religious community's remaining attentive before the revelations of the arts, and particularly of the arts of language. For the poets—that is, the artists of language—are the most sensitive seismographs of the times; they are apt to be the first to register the profound tides that move society and culture. They are the sensitive ones who first register and react to changes in the climate. They fish in deep waters and bring to light evidence from the inner world and the underworld by a kind of divination, evidence which we may well take into account. This is a part of the mystery of the word. On the one hand there is the power of the word to create new worlds and destroy old, and the new poets are at it today as poets have always been. But there is the attendant and perhaps prior power of the word to get hold of yet obscure meanings and directions and values, and crystallize them. The new poets are doing that today.[16]

And this is why their work must be studied closely. For in such modern books as Franz Kafka's *The Castle,* Elias Canetti's *Auto da Fé,* William Faulkner's *Light in August,* Jean-Paul Sartre's *Nausea,* Robert Penn Warren's *All the King's Men,* and Malcolm Lowry's *Under the Volcano* we behold the full body of our time, and, in doing so, we peer into the dark, secret labyrinths of ourselves. We regard ourselves "as it were at second hand . . . refracted into *personae* (masks) of . . . [our] condition *with the masks removed!"* [17] We are not, to be sure, thereby *engaged* by any moral or religious imperative, for, as we have observed, the poetic experience does not terminate in *commitment;* and yet, as it has been argued here, the ultimate religious commitments that we must finally undertake are not likely to be entered into with discretion if we are without the insights that that experience affords. This is, I think, what Professor Stanley Hopper means when he tells us in his fine book *The Crisis of Faith* that "poetry will not save the world. But poetry can force the soul into the precincts of its last evasion." [18]

There is an English lady who writes as a poet and a critic and who remarked a few years ago of Kafka that she had always had the feeling that "he is, with enormous effort, getting from somewhere that I have never been, to somewhere else that I would not want to go to anyway." And this is likely, I suspect, to be the testimony of those who resist that insulation of the ego from itself which is the means by which great literature forces us into the precincts of our last evasions. We should, most of us, like to think that "conditions" and our own souls are not in the wretched plight in which so many of the great writers of our day have implied that they are. Indeed, we tell ourselves that things mightn't even be so bad as they are were our literary artists not so insistent upon the unsatisfactoriness of modern life; we often naïvely suppose, as Mr. Allen Tate has noticed, that "there would be no hell for modern man if our men of letters were not calling attention to it." [19] And so we believe that where Joyce and Kafka and Faulkner and Malraux have come from is a place to which we have never been and that where they go is a place whose terrain we could not possibly recognize. But this is the pathetic illogic of the self-deceived and of those who would evade the awful embarrassment that overtakes us in the moment of confession which is the moment to which the great poets finally bring us. For, in making us see ourselves, they make us see that we are less than what we should and might be. This is not a moment of *decision* but a moment of *discovery;* yet what we must see is that the *decisions* which high religion elicits may not be made with the fullest sense of the human realities upon which they bear if they are uninformed by that deep knowledge of the human condition which the poetic experience affords and which is its great gift to the spiritual life.

There will, of course, doubtless always be a certain degree of tension between art and religion, for, as Mr. Allen Tate has said, "The subject of the imaginative writer is necessarily men as they are behaving, not as they ought to behave." And thus there is likely to be, as Mr. Tate says, "a standing quarrel between the imaginative writer and the Church." [20] But the antagonism—however much it may not really be ultimately necessitated in principle (and Mr. Tate is actually thinking not so much of *art* and *religion* as absolute essences as he is of *the artist* and *the churchman*)—is by no means so rigidly joined today as it was at an earlier time. This is particularly noticeable in the world of Protestantism, whose historic affiliation with bourgeois attitudes has traditionally conditioned it toward a certain skepticism of literature and the arts. This skepticism was never well founded, being rooted not so much in theological principles as in a comfortable social-economic situation that closeted the Protestant consciousness from the bitter realities of the iron time which the modern artist was exploring. But the events of recent history have not only broken an earlier complacency about the human enterprise but have also compelled us to undertake deeper explorations of the meaning of the Christian faith itself—so that, the full implications of Gethsemane having been repossessed, the austere and tragic vision of the great poets and novelists of our period is no longer the offense that it once was.

The new congeniality in the religious community toward the testimony of modern literature has also in large part, I suspect, been a result of the emergence of a significant Christian literature out of the epochal agonies of the time. In the English-speaking world alone we have today the very remarkable constellation of such writers as T. S. Eliot, Edith Sitwell, W. H. Auden, Graham Greene, Robert Lowell, and (possibly we ought also to include) the late Dylan Thomas. Mr. Graham Greene has distinguished between those writers who merely happen to be Christians and those who are genuinely Christian writers in the sense that their way, as artists, of shaping the substance of experience is determined by an essentially Christian vision of things. And it is amongst this latter group that the writers whom I have mentioned, in some degree or other, belong. They are, or at least they seek to be, in this integral way, Christian artists. And their example has been so gratifying till they have won a wide and devoted audience throughout the Christian community, amongst Anglican, Protestant, and Roman Catholic readers. Indeed, the great danger perhaps is that, having given to their work the initially warm response that it deserved, we may now, out of sympathy with their minority position in the larger culture, be failing to practice the kind of tact in discrimination that might result in the more careful assessments for which their books begin to ask. We have, I suspect, been so busy in congratulating both them and ourselves on what is called *the Christian renascence in literature* that we have neglected to take a proper measure of the difficulties involved in being a Christian artist and of whether such a thing is, after all, really possible in our time, at least in the degree that we often assume to have been realized.

What we have, I think, to take into account is that in order for the Christian writer (or, indeed, for that matter, any other Christian worker in the field of culture) to assert his identity in the modern world, it has been necessary for him to do so *against* his environment and his culture, for there Christianity has been, on the whole, at a discount. Till only the day before yesterday the dominant religion ever since the sixteenth century had been the religion of progress, with its vision of history automatically moving toward ever wider and wider harmonies and toward the perfection of the natural man. And in such a climate the inevitable posture of the Christian writer had to be that of being *against* his environment: his primary impulse was, inevitably, to dwell upon those aspects of Christian orthodoxy the emphatic assertion of which might have the effect of correcting or of calling into question the dominant heresies of the age. In the modern world the approach, in other words, of the Christian writer to his faith has tended to be governed by strategic considerations. And this has in turn very often resulted in his representing himself an imbalance that was but the opposite of the imbalance which he found in his culture. He has wanted, say, in opposition to the complacencies of modern culture, to reinstate a sense of the human tragedy and of man's radical imperfection and limitation. And so, with great exertion, he has undertaken to recover for his age a sense of the straits that man is permanently in, of his need for redemption, and of what the Church has traditionally meant by the *originality* of sin. But, in the process of disclosing to us how deeply wounded the human creature is and how narrowly his life escapes being engulfed by the terrible vacuums of tragedy, the Christian writer has often seemed to forget that things were, though, made right and valid in Christ, in his Passion and in his Resurrection. The emphasis, in other words, upon a single aspect of the Christian testimony is so drastic as to provide an example of what the Church has indeed traditionally conceived heresy to involve. Or, to put it differently, we do not get a central or an integral version of the Christian understanding of human existence.

The fiction of Mr. William Faulkner here provides us with a kind of case in point. Just as *Ash Wednesday* and the *Quartets* have helped us to see that the author of *The Waste Land* and *The Hollow Men* was in many ways essentially a poet Christianly oriented, whatever may then have been the state of his relations with the Church, so too "The Bear" and *Requiem for a Nun* and *A Fable* have helped us to make a similar discovery about the author of *Sartoris* and *The Sound and the Fury* and *Absalom, Absalom!* Surely we ought by now to be able to forget all the nonsense that used to be talked about Mr. Faulkner as a novelist of Southern "decadence" and to take seriously one of his finest critics, Mr. R. W. B. Lewis, who tells us that the world into which we are taken by his books is the "world after the Incarnation." [21] It is true, of course, that, unlike Mr. Eliot and Mr. Auden, Mr. Faulkner has no great capacity for handling systematic ideas with cogency—but he has an enormous cogency where for him it really counts, namely, in the dialectical entanglements of his fiction. And here the observable consistencies (in the delineation of character and the management of narrative perspective) suggest that, at the very least, his is a mind that is inclinatorily Christian. Yet the stress of it is toward a pessimism at times so unremitting as to recall the world *before* the Incarnation, of Aeschylus and Sophocles. Indeed, it is significant, as I have noted in an earlier chapter (and as others have elsewhere done), that the very words to which he has to return again and again are "tragic," "inexorable," "intractable," and "outrage." He brings before us "the tragic and inevitable land," a doomed and accursed place in which the exigencies of life are often beyond human endurance; yet, according to the logic of his moral universe, it is only when man is pitted against such odds that he discovers in himself the capacity to endure anything at all. Mr. Faulkner, in other words, has wanted to make our griefs grieve on universal bones—and the point is that in the very process of awakening us out of our specious securities he has himself lost the kind of centrality of vision that might enable us to regard his own sensibility as integrally Christian.

Or, again, a similar imbalance is discoverable in Mr. Graham Greene. Mr. Greene's relation to Christianity is, to be sure, more highly formalized than Mr. Faulkner's, but we do not find, *in his novels,* a Christian sensibility that represents any greater degree of balance or integration. He is a Christian writer who has wanted in much of his work to exhibit the moral and spiritual superficiality of the modern secularist consciousness, with its shallow preoccupation with Right and Wrong and its ignorance of Good and Evil. And Mr. Greene's own preoccupations have often reminded us of the great passage in Mr. Eliot's essay on Baudelaire in which he says: "So far as we are human, what we do must be either evil or good; so far as we do evil or good we are human; and it is better, in a paradoxical way, to do evil than to do nothing; at least, we exist. . . . The worst that can be said of most of our malefactors . . . is that they are not men enough to be damned." [22] And, wanting to demonstrate this, Mr. Greene has tended to find the great thing in many of his characters—in (to name only a few) Minty in *England Made Me,* or Pinkie in *Brighton Rock,* or Fowler in *The Quiet American*—to be their intimate knowledge of Evil: however reprehensible they might be, he has expected us to find in them a human profundity that is missing in Wilson of *The Heart of the Matter* or in Pyle of *The Quiet American,* who, though conventionally upright in their morals, do not have, in their consciousness merely of what is Right and Wrong, sufficient substance to be damned. As Scott Fitzgerald suggested, in that famous rejoinder to Mr. Ernest Hemingway, there are some who represent the authority of success and others who represent the authority of failure, and it is the latter in whom Mr. Greene is chiefly interested. So we get in many of his books a commitment to a kind of romantic diabolism that seems rather curiously to betray the Christian position to which he offers his conscious suffrage. Again, in other words, we see how costly it is for the artist to undertake an orthodox position in our heterodox world. For, as he takes this kind of anchorage, he is led, by the circumstances of his time, to try to correct the historical imbalance, and, in doing so, he is often betrayed into so drastic an emphasis upon some particular insight of the Christian faith that he himself loses the kind of centrality that in a happier period he might achieve.

Instead, then, of merely assuming a proprietary air about *the Christian renascence in literature* today, perhaps it is with discriminations such as these that the Christian reader ought to begin to concern himself, for they are to be made—and far more extensively than I have indicated here—with respect to many other leading writers of our time. The truth of the matter is, after all, that their work has been

> forged beneath the hammer of truth
> On the anvil of our anguish.[23]

And what it therefore requires is not any form of adulatory enshrinement—which would, in any event, hardly be a sufficiently active response to it—but rather the most rigorous questioning to which it can be submitted by the faith in which both we and its authors find the greatest illumination of the deep places of human life. And if we succeed in bringing the Christian faith into a genuinely dialogical relationship with modern literature, so that art may speak to religion and religion to art, we may in due time get a renewal and a deepening of both.

Notes

Preface

[1] Paul Tillich, *The Protestant Era* (Chicago: University of Chicago Press, 1948), p. xiii.

[2] Paul Tillich, *Systematic Theology* (Chicago: University of Chicago Press, 1951), Vol. I, pp. 61–62.

[3] *Ibid.*, p. 63.

[4] *Ibid.*, p. 64.

[5] Stanley R. Hopper in Editor's Foreword, *Spiritual Problems in Contemporary Literature* (New York: Harper & Brothers, 1952), p. xi.

[6] *Ibid.*, p. xiii.

Chapter I
Poetry, Religion, and the Modern Mind

[1] Alfred C. Kinsey, Wardell B. Pomeroy, and Clyde E. Martin, *Sexual Behavior in the Human Male* (Philadelphia: W. B. Saunders Co., 1948).

[2] Lionel Trilling, *The Liberal Imagination* (New York: Viking Press, 1950), p. 235.

[3] Winston H. F. Barnes, *The Philosophical Predicament* (Boston: Beacon Press, 1950), p. 17.

[4] *Ibid.*, p. 101.

[5] Lancelot Hogben, *The Nature of Living Matter* (London: Kegan Paul, Ltd., 1947), p. 261.

[6] Barnes, *op. cit.*, p. 119.

[7] Alfred J. Ayer, *Language, Truth and Logic* (London: Victor Gollancz Ltd., 1953 [ninth impression of the second edition]), p. 110.

[8] *Ibid.*, p. 41.

[9] Herbert Muller, *Science and Criticism* (New Haven: Yale University Press, 1943), pp. 90–95.

[10] Basil Willey, *The Seventeenth Century Background* (London: Chatto and Windus, 1934), *passim*.

[11] L. C. Knights, "Bacon and the Seventeenth Century Dissociation of Sensibility," in *Explorations* (New York: George W. Stewart, Inc., 1947).

[12] Willey, *op. cit.*, p. 87.

[13] *Ibid.*, p. 301.

[14] John Crowe Ransom, *The World's Body* (New York: Charles Scribner's Sons, 1938), p. 135.

[15] Willey, *op. cit.,* p. 87.

[16] *Ibid.*

[17] Michael Roberts, *The Modern Mind* (London: Faber and Faber, Ltd., 1937), p. 102.

[18] Willey, *op. cit.,* p. 297.

[19] Ransom, *op. cit.,* p. 135.

[20] T. S. Eliot, "The Metaphysical Poets," in *Selected Essays: 1917–1932* (New York: Harcourt, Brace and Co., 1932).

[21] Willey, *op. cit.,* p. 279.

[22] *Letters of Samuel Taylor Coleridge,* ed. Ernest Hartley Coleridge (2 vols.; London, 1895), Vol. I, p. 352.

[23] Samuel Taylor Coleridge, *Biographia Literaria,* ed. J. Shawcross (2 vols.; London: Oxford University Press, 1907), Vol. I, p. 202.

[24] Samuel Taylor Coleridge, review of poems of Drake and Halleck in *Southern Literary Messenger,* April, 1836.

[25] C. M. Bowra, *The Romantic Imagination* (Cambridge: Harvard University Press, 1949), p. 23.

[26] T. S. Eliot, "Arnold and Pater," *op. cit.,* p. 351.

[27] T. S. Eliot, *The Use of Poetry and the Use of Criticism* (London: Faber and Faber, Ltd., 1933), p. 129.

[28] Cleanth Brooks, "Metaphor and the Function of Criticism," in *Spiritual Problems in Contemporary Literature,* ed. Stanley R. Hopper (New York: Harper & Brothers, 1952), p. 134.

[29] Cleanth Brooks, *The Well Wrought Urn* (London: Dennis Dobson Ltd., n.d. [Originally published in New York by Reynal and Hitchcock in 1947]), p. 233.

[30] Wilbur Marshall Urban, *Language and Reality* (London: George Allen and Unwin, Ltd., 1951), p. 500.

[31] Allen Tate, *On the Limits of Poetry* (New York: Swallow Press and W. Morrow and Co., 1948), p. 4.

[32] Amos N. Wilder, *Modern Poetry and the Christian Tradition* (New York: Charles Scribner's Sons, 1952), p. xi.

[33] Paul Tillich, *The Protestant Era* (Chicago: University of Chicago Press, 1948), p. 58.

[34] Urban, *op. cit.,* pp. 498–502.

[35] The phrase is used by Cleanth Brooks in "Metaphor and the Function of Criticism," *op. cit.,* pp. 131–132.

[36] Wilder, *op. cit.,* p. 259.

[37] *Ibid.,* p. xii.

[38] *Ibid.,* p. 243.

[39] *Ibid.,* p. 244.

Chapter II
The Modern Experiment in Criticism: A Theological Appraisal

[1] The reference is to Mr. Tate's essay "Is Literary Criticism Possible?" which appears in his book *The Forlorn Demon: Didactic and Critical Essays* (Chicago: Henry Regnery Co., 1953).

[2] Ernst Cassirer, *Language and Myth,* trans. Susanne K. Langer (New York: Harper & Brothers, 1946), p. 91.

[3] Cleanth Brooks, "Irony as a Principle of Structure," in *Literary Opinion in America,* ed. Morton Dauwen Zabel (New York: Harper & Brothers, 1951), pp. 730–731.

[4] Cleanth Brooks, *The Well Wrought Urn* (London: Dennis Dobson Ltd., n.d. [Originally published in New York by Reynal and Hitchcock in 1947]), p. 188.

[5] Joseph Frank, "Spatial Form in Modern Literature," in *Criticism: The Foundations of Modern Literary Judgment,* ed. Mark Schorer *et al.* (New York: Harcourt, Brace and Co., 1948), p. 383. Mr. Frank's essay contains some very acute observations upon the "reflexive" character of poetic language.

[6] Brooks, *op. cit.,* p. 186.

[7] Ezra Pound, "Epstein, Belgion and Meaning," *The Criterion,* Vol. IX, No. XXXVI (April, 1930), p. 471.

[8] Denis de Rougemont, "Religion and the Mission of the Artist," in *Spiritual Problems in Contemporary Literature,* ed. Stanley R. Hopper (New York: Harper & Brothers, 1952), p. 177.

[9] *Vide* Eliseo Vivas, "A Definition of the Esthetic Experience," in *The Problems of Aesthetics,* ed. Eliseo Vivas and Murray Krieger (New York: Rinehart and Co., 1953), pp. 406–411. It is to Professor Vivas that we are indebted for the definition in contemporary aesthetics of the poetic experience in terms of "intransitive attention." This concept receives further elaboration in his book *Creation and Discovery* (New York: Noonday Press, 1955).

[10] Cleanth Brooks, *Modern Poetry and the Tradition* (Chapel Hill: University of North Carolina Press, 1939), p. 43.

[11] T. S. Eliot, "Preface to the 1928 Edition," *The Sacred Wood* (London: Faber and Faber Ltd., 1934, 4th ed.), pp. ix–x.

[12] Murray Krieger, *The New Apologists for Poetry* (Minneapolis: University of Minnesota Press, 1956), p. 23.

[13] R. P. Blackmur, "The Craft of Herman Melville: A Putative Statement," in *The Lion and the Honeycomb* (New York: Harcourt, Brace and Co., 1955), p. 138.

[14] Mark Van Doren, *The Noble Voice* (New York: Henry Holt and Co., 1946), pp. 181–182.

[15] I. A. Richards, *The Philosophy of Rhetoric* (New York: Oxford University Press, 1936), p. 131.

[16] D. S. Savage, *The Withered Branch* (New York: Pellegrini and Cudahy, n.d.), p. 12.

[17] In the following account of this book that I give I have liberally raided two of the pages in an article of mine ("Maritain in His Role as Aesthetician") that appeared in *The Review of Metaphysics* in March, 1955 (Vol. VIII, No. 3). I am indebted to the editor, Professor Paul Weiss, for permitting this act of plunderage.

[18] Jacques Maritain, *Creative Intuition in Art and Poetry* (New York: Pantheon Books, 1953), p. 62.

[19] *Ibid.,* p. 239.

[20] *Ibid.*

[21] *Ibid.,* p. 243.

[22] *Ibid.,* p. 223.

[23] *Ibid.*, p. 63.

[24] *Ibid.*, p. 60.

[25] *Ibid.*, p. 126.

[26] *Ibid.*

[27] *Ibid.*, p. 246.

[28] *Ibid.*, p. 218.

[29] Vivas, *Creation and Discovery*, p. 117.

[30] Henry James, *The Art of the Novel: Critical Prefaces* (New York: Charles Scribner's Sons, 1934), p. 5.

[31] Graham Greene, *The Lost Childhood* (New York: Viking Press, 1952), p. 79.

[32] Martin Jarrett-Kerr, *Studies in Literature and Belief* (New York: Harper & Brothers, 1955), p. 5.

[33] W. K. Wimsatt and Monroe Beardsley, "The Intentional Fallacy," *The Sewanee Review*, Vol. LIV (Summer, 1946), pp. 468–488.

[34] Vivas, *op. cit.*, p. 172.

[35] *Ibid.*

[36] *Ibid.*, p. 164.

[37] De Rougemont, *op. cit.*, p. 176.

[38] Paul Tillich, *The Protestant Era* (Chicago: University of Chicago Press, 1948), p. 57.

[39] Paul Tillich, *The Interpretation of History* (New York: Charles Scribner's Sons, 1936), p. 49.

[40] Tillich, *The Protestant Era*, p. 57.

[41] *Ibid.*, p. 59.

[42] *Ibid.*, pp. 58–59.

[43] T. S. Eliot, *Notes Towards the Definition of Culture* (New York: Harcourt, Brace and Co., 1949), pp. 31–32.

[44] James Luther Adams, "Tillich's Concept of the Protestant Era," Editor's Appendix, *The Protestant Era*, p. 273.

[45] M. de Rougemont says that "art would appear to be like an invocation (more often than not unconscious) to the lost harmony, like a prayer (more often than not confused), corresponding to the second petition of the Lord's Prayer—'Thy Kingdom come.'" *Vide op. cit.*, p. 186.

[46] Leslie Fiedler, "Toward an Amateur Criticism," *The Kenyon Review*, Vol. XII, No. 4 (Autumn, 1950), p. 564.

[47] S. L. Bethell, *Essays on Literary Criticism and the English Tradition* (London: Dennis Dobson Ltd., 1948), pp. 24–25.

[48] *Ibid.*, p. 25.

[49] Roy W. Battenhouse, "The Relation of Theology to Literary Criticism," *The Journal of Bible and Religion*, Vol. XIII, No. 1 (February, 1945), p. 20.

[50] *Ibid.*

[51] Erich Heller, *The Disinherited Mind: Essays in Modern German Literature and Thought* (Philadelphia: Dufour and Saifer, 1952), p. 125.

[52] Eliot, *op. cit.*, p. 29.

[53] Amos N. Wilder, *Modern Poetry and the Christian Tradition* (New York: Charles Scribner's Sons, 1952), p. 176.

[54] *Ibid.*, p. 268.

[55] *Ibid.*

[56] *Ibid.*, p. 243.

[57] Amos N. Wilder, *The Spiritual Aspects of the New Poetry* (New York: Harper & Brothers, 1940), pp. 197–198.

[58] *Vide* Wilder, *Modern Poetry and the Christian Tradition*, Chapter X.

[59] Wilder, *The Spiritual Aspects of the New Poetry*, p. 196.

[60] Wladimir Weidlé, *The Dilemma of the Arts*, trans. by Martin Jarrett-Kerr (London: S.C.M. Press Ltd., 1948), Chapter VI.

[61] Tillich, *The Protestant Era*, pp. 56–57.

[62] *Ibid.*, p. xvi.

[63] *Ibid.*

[64] Weidlé, *op. cit.*, p. 125.

Chapter III
Prolegomenon to a Christian Poetic

[1] Martin Buber, *I and Thou* (Edinburgh: T. and T. Clark, 1937), p. 60.

[2] *Ibid.*, p. 61.

[3] *Ibid.*, p. 62.

[4] *Ibid.*, p. 64.

[5] *Ibid.*

[6] *Ibid.*, p. 65.

[7] *Ibid.*, p. 15.

[8] *Ibid.*, p. 4.

[9] Philip Wheelwright, *The Burning Fountain: A Study in the Language of Symbolism* (Bloomington: Indiana University Press, 1954), p. 81.

[10] The phrase "spiritually responsive" universe is borrowed from Wheelwright; *vide ibid.*, pp. 290–296.

[11] Quoted *ibid.*, pp. 78–79.

[12] Psalm 148.

[13] Allen Tate, *The Forlorn Demon: Didactic and Critical Essays* (Chicago: Henry Regnery Co., 1953), p. 36.

[14] *Vide* Charles Williams, *The Figure of Beatrice: A Study in Dante* (London: Faber and Faber Ltd., 1943), pp. 7–16.

[15] A phrase which Professor Hodges used in an address on "Art and Religion" that was delivered to the Chelmsford Diocesan Worship and the Arts Association, meeting at St. Hugh's College, Oxford, July 14, 1947.

[16] Williams, *op. cit.*, p. 44.

[17] The phrase is Stanley R. Hopper's: *vide* his "The Problem of Moral Isolation in Contemporary Literature," in the volume of his editorship *Spiritual Problems in Contemporary Literature* (New York: Harper & Brothers, 1952), p. 162.

[18] William Temple, *Nature, Man and God* (New York: The Macmillan Company, 1934), p. 57.

[19] Tate, *op. cit.*, pp. 4–5.

[20] Jacques Maritain, *The Dream of Descartes* (New York: Philosophical Library, 1944), p. 180.

[21] Tate, *op. cit.*, p. 68.

[22] *Vide* Chapter IV ("The Cartesian Heritage") in Maritain, *op. cit.*; *vide* also Chapters III ("The Symbolic Imagination: The Mirrors of Dante") and IV ("The Angelic Imagination: Poe as God") in Tate, *op. cit.* My debt to both M. Maritain and Mr. Tate is enormous.

[23] Raissa Maritain, "Magic, Poetry, and Mysticism," *The Situation of Poetry* (New York: Philosophical Library, 1955), p. 24.

[24] Translated by Louise Varèse and included as a part of the Preface to her edition of Rimbaud's *Illuminations* (New York: New Directions, 1946), pp. xxvi–xxvii.

[25] Wallace Fowlie, *Rimbaud* (New York: New Directions, 1946), p. 99.

[26] Jacques Maritain, *Creative Intuition in Art and Poetry* (New York: Pantheon Books, 1953), p. 189.

[27] T. S. Eliot, "From Poe to Valéry," *Hudson Review*, Vol. I, No. 3 (Autumn, 1949), p. 340.

[28] Maritain, *op. cit.*, p. 78.

[29] Wladimir Weidlé, *The Dilemma of the Arts*, trans. by Martin Jarrett-Kerr (London: S. C. M. Press Ltd., 1948), p. 65.

[30] Denis de Rougemont, "Religion and the Mission of the Artist," *Spiritual Problems in Contemporary Literature*, ed. Stanley R. Hopper (New York: Harper & Brothers, 1952), p. 174.

[31] *Ibid.*, pp. 183–185.

[32] Edmund Wilson, *The Triple Thinkers* (New York: Oxford University Press, 1948), p. 25.

[33] Weidlé, *op. cit.*, p. 98.

[34] Tate, *op. cit.*, p. 37.

[35] Douglas Knight, *Religious Implications in the Humanities* (Hazen Pamphlets, No. 27, New Haven: Edward W. Hazen Foundation, 1951), p. 7.

[36] Edwin Muir, *Essays on Literature and Society* (London: Hogarth Press, 1949), p. 144.

[37] Erich Auerbach, *Mimesis* (Princeton: Princeton University Press, 1953), p. 538.

[38] Robert G. Cohn, "Sartre's First Novel: *La Nausée,*" *Yale French Studies*, Vol. I, No. 1 (Spring-Summer, 1948), p. 62.

[39] Iris Murdoch, *Sartre: Romantic Rationalist* (New Haven: Yale University Press, 1953), p. 25.

[40] *Ibid.*

[41] William F. Lynch, "Theology and the Imagination," *Thought*, Vol. XXIX, No. 112 (Spring, 1954), p. 67.

[42] J. V. Langmead Casserley, *The Christian in Philosophy* (London: Faber and Faber Ltd., 1949), p. 59.

[43] The reader will, I assume, by now have noticed that throughout this whole section of our discussion I am greatly indebted to the thought of Professor Paul Tillich, and particularly to three of his recent books—*The Protestant Era* (Chicago: University of Chicago Press, 1948), *Systematic Theology*, Vol. I (Chicago: University of Chicago Press, 1951), and *The Courage to Be* (New Haven: Yale University Press, 1952). There is perhaps no other major Christian philosopher of our day—possibly with the exception of Mr. Langmead Casserley —who has perceived with such penetration as Dr. Tillich the true implications and the profound relevance of the ontologism native to those traditions of philosophy that have their ultimate source in the Christian existentialism of Augustine. And my formulations throughout the latter section of this chapter are fundamentally derivative from his; indeed, at several points I have taken over his special terminology—as, for example, in my use of such terms as "Being-

itself," "the Ground of Being," "the New Testament picture of Jesus as the Christ," "the Unconditional," etc. In the text these terms are not set apart by inverted commas, but my readers will, of course, recognize their actual source.

44 Tillich, *Systematic Theology,* Vol. I, p. 251.

45 *Vide* especially in this connection his article "A Reinterpretation of the Doctrine of the Incarnation," in the *Church Quarterly Review,* Vol. 147, No. 294 (January-March, 1949).

46 Lynch, *op. cit.,* pp. 72–73. Certainly, in cataloguing my indebtments in these notes, I must not omit mention of Fr. Lynch, who, in his brilliant essays of recent years in *Thought* (the Fordham University quarterly of which he was formerly the editor), has shown himself to belong to those Roman Catholic writers—amongst whom I have in mind Jacques and Raissa Maritain and Allen Tate—who have seen most clearly the predicament of the modern poet and who, in their analysis of it, have helped to make available to us all much of the wisdom of the *central* Christian tradition. Fr. Lynch's Thomist commitments, however—for the reasons that, as a matter of *principle,* I have suggested—prevent his *prescriptions* with respect to the ontological problem from having the relevancy that is finally required.

47 Tillich, *The Protestant Era,* p. xiv.

Chapter IV
Man in Recent Literature

1 W. H. Auden, *The Enchafèd Flood* (New York: Random House, 1950), p. 66.

2 T. S. Eliot, "Ulysses, Order, and Myth," in *Forms of Modern Fiction,* ed. William Van O'Connor (Minneapolis: University of Minnesota Press, 1948), p. 123.

3 Alfred Kazin, *On Native Grounds* (New York: Reynal and Hitchcock, 1942), p. 451.

4 Karl Shapiro, *Essay on Rime* (New York: Reynal and Hitchcock, 1945), p. 63.

5 *Vide* William Van O'Connor's discussion of Crane in this connection in his *Sense and Sensibility in Modern Poetry* (Chicago: University of Chicago Press, 1948), Chapter II.

6 Philip Wheelwright, "Poetry, Myth, and Reality," in *The Language of Poetry,* ed. Allen Tate (Princeton: Princeton University Press, 1942), p. 32.

7 Nathan A. Scott, Jr., *Rehearsals of Discomposure: Alienation and Reconciliation in Modern Literature* (New York: King's Crown Press of Columbia University Press, 1952), p. 7.

8 Lionel Trilling, *The Liberal Imagination* (New York: Viking Press, 1950), p. 270.

9 *Ibid.*

10 Stanley R. Hopper, *The Crisis of Faith* (Nashville: Abingdon-Cokesbury Press, 1944), p. 15.

11 Diana Trilling, "Editor's Introduction," *The Portable D. H. Lawrence* (New York: Viking Press, 1947), p. 13.

12 *Ibid.*

13 Jean-Paul Sartre, *What Is Literature?* (New York: Philosophical Library, 1949), p. 222.

[14] F. O. Matthiessen, *From the Heart of Europe* (New York: Oxford University Press, 1948), pp. 45–46.

[15] Mr. Wallace Fowlie, in discussing Rimbaud, has spoken of "the Myth of Hell" and "the Myth of Voyage" in the beautifully executed little book which he has devoted to that poet (*Rimbaud* [New York: New Directions, 1946]), and it is from him that I borrow a part of my phraseology.

[16] *Vide* Amos N. Wilder, *The Spiritual Aspects of the New Poetry* (New York: Harper & Brothers, 1940), Chapter VIII, "A World Without Roots."

[17] The English critic, Mr. J. Isaacs, in his book *An Assessment of Twentieth-Century Literature* (London: Secker and Warburg, 1951), has written suggestively of the symbolic uses to which the image of "the City" has been put in modern literature.

[18] Wallace Fowlie, *Jacob's Night: The Religious Renascence in France* (New York: Sheed and Ward, 1947), p. 42.

[19] The phrase is used by Mr. Fowlie in a characterization of the modern artist in his book on Rimbaud (*op. cit.*, p. 111).

[20] W. H. Auden, "Yeats as an Example," in *The Permanence of Yeats*, ed. D. Hall and M. Steinmann (New York: The Macmillan Company, 1950), p. 348.

[21] Archibald Fleming, "The Destroyers," *The New Republic*, July 13, 1938, p. 273.

[22] Dante, *The Divine Comedy*, trans. Laurence Binyon, ed. Paolo Milano (New York: Viking Press, 1948), "Inferno," III, 57.

[23] *Vide* Malcolm Cowley, "An Introduction to William Faulkner," *Critiques and Essays on Modern Fiction: 1920–1951*, ed. John W. Aldridge (New York: Ronald Press, 1952), pp. 427–446.

[24] Irving Howe, *William Faulkner: A Critical Study* (New York: Random House, 1952), pp. 21–22.

[25] *Ibid.*, p. 23.

[26] *Ibid.*, p. 104.

[27] Reinhold Niebuhr, *Discerning the Signs of the Times* (New York: Charles Scribner's Sons, 1946). *Vide* Chapter III.

[28] W. H. Auden, "Petition," *The Collected Poetry* (New York: Random House, 1945), p. 111.

[29] *Ibid.*, p. 110.

[30] W. H. Auden, "K.'s Quest," in *The Kafka Problem*, ed. Angel Flores (New York: New Directions, 1946), p. 49.

[31] Richard Hoggart, *Auden: An Introductory Essay* (New Haven: Yale University Press, 1951), p. 170.

[32] Louise Bogan, "Putting to Sea," *The Sleeping Fury* (New York: Charles Scribner's Sons, 1937), pp. 36–37.

[33] William Butler Yeats, "Byzantium," *The Collected Poems* (New York: The Macmillan Company, 1951), p. 244.

[34] Stanley R. Hopper, "The Problem of Moral Isolation in Contemporary Literature," *Spiritual Problems in Contemporary Literature* (New York: Harper & Brothers, 1952), p. 154.

[35] A frequently repeated phrase in the poetry of W. H. Auden: the poet's reference is to the precincts within which beatitude is to be had, to "the Place of Love," but this "Place," perhaps inevitably, never gains sharp definition.

[36] T. S. Eliot, "Burnt Norton," *Four Quartets* (New York: Harcourt, Brace and Co., 1943), p. 5.

[37] "The Ascent of Mt. Carmel," *The Complete Works of Saint John of the Cross,* trans. from the critical edition of P. Silverio de Santa Teresa, C.D., and ed. Ellison Peers (London: Burns, Oates and Washbourne, Ltd., 1934), Vol. I, pp. 19–20.

[38] T. S. Eliot, *The Family Reunion* (New York: Harcourt, Brace and Co., 1939), p. III.

[39] Eliot, "Burnt Norton," *Four Quartets,* p. 6.

[40] Norman Nicholson, "T. S. Eliot," in *Writers of Today,* ed. Denys Val Baker (London: Sidgwick and Jackson, 1946), p. 142.

[41] Eliot, "East Coker," *Four Quartets,* p. 15.

[42] Auden, "New Year Letter," *The Collected Poetry,* p. 272.

[43] *Ibid.*

[44] Eliot, "East Coker," *Four Quartets,* p. 14.

[45] Eliot, "The Dry Salvages," *Four Quartets,* pp. 25–26.

[46] T. E. Hulme, *Speculations,* ed. Herbert Read (London: Kegan Paul, Trench, Trubner and Co., Ltd., 1936), p. 4.

[47] *Vide* Chapter III, note 17.

[48] Nicodemus, *Renascence: An Essay in Faith* (London: Faber and Faber, Ltd., 1943), p. 65.

[49] T. S. Eliot, "Dante," *Selected Essays: 1917–1932* (New York: Harcourt, Brace and Co., 1932), p. 214.

Chapter V
The Personal Principle: A Conspectus of the Poetic and Religious Vision at the Present Time

[1] T. S. Eliot, "East Coker," *Four Quartets* (New York: Harcourt, Brace and Co., 1943), p. 15.

[2] Gabriel Marcel, *Homo Viator* (Chicago: Henry Regnery Co., 1951), p. 213.

[3] Rainer Maria Rilke, *Letters to a Young Poet* (New York: W. W. Norton and Co., 1934), pp. 33–34.

[4] Edna St. Vincent Millay, *Conversation at Midnight* (New York: Harper & Brothers, 1937), p. 27.

[5] Marcel, *op. cit.,* p. 134.

[6] Boston: Little, Brown and Co., 1951.

[7] *The London Magazine,* Vol. III, No. 12 (December, 1956), p. 75.

[8] *Vide* Malcolm Cowley, *The Literary Situation* (New York: Viking Press, 1954), Chapter V.

[9] Henry Reed, *The Novel Since 1939* (London: Published for the British Council by Longmans, Green and Co., 1946), p. 23.

[10] Lionel Trilling, *The Liberal Imagination* (New York: Viking Press, 1950), p. 266.

[11] Cowley, *op. cit.,* p. 54.

[12] W. H. Auden, "New Year Letter," *The Collected Poetry* (New York: Random House, 1945), p. 272.

[13] Albert J. Guerard, "The Ivory Tower and the Dust Bowl," *New World Writing,* No. 3, p. 353.

[14] Max Lerner, "The Human Voyage," in *The Kafka Problem,* ed. Angel Flores (New York: New Directions, 1946), p. 42.

[15] Dorothy M. Emmet, *The Nature of Metaphysical Thinking* (London: Macmillan and Co., Ltd., 1949), p. 223.

[16] Lerner, *op. cit.,* p. 44.

[17] Gabriel Marcel, *The Mystery of Being* (Chicago: Henry Regnery Co., 1950), Vol. I, p. 28.

[18] *Vide* Cowley, *op. cit.,* Chapter III.

[19] Robert Gorham Davis, "In a Raveled World Love Endures," *The New York Times Book Review,* December 26, 1954, p. 13.

[20] J. V. Langmead Casserley, "Gabriel Marcel," in *Christianity and the Existentialists,* ed. Carl Michalson (New York: Charles Scribner's Sons, 1956), p. 88.

[21] Trilling, *op. cit.,* p. xii.

[22] Harry Slochower, *No Voice Is Wholly Lost* (New York: Creative Age Press, Inc., 1945), p. 323.

[23] Langmead Casserley, *op. cit.,* p. 88.

Chapter VI
Beneath the Hammer of Truth

[1] *Vide* Paul Tillich, *The Protestant Era* (Chicago: University of Chicago Press, 1948), Sections II, III, and IV.

[2] By the term "poetry" I mean all the high forms of imaginative literature—the poet, I take it, being every writer (not simply the writer in verse but also the novelist and the dramatist) who handles language with such artistry that we are compelled to perform before his work an act of rapt attention.

[3] Allen Tate, *On the Limits of Poetry* (New York: Swallow Press and W. Morrow & Co., 1948), p. xi.

[4] *Vide* under Chapter II, note 11.

[5] *Vide* under Chapter II, note 9.

[6] Susanne K. Langer, *Philosopher in a New Key* (New York: New American Library, 1948), p. 212.

[7] Samuel Taylor Coleridge, *Biographia Literaria,* ed. J. Shawcross (London: Oxford University Press, 1907), Vol. II, p. 12.

[8] My terms again are Professor Eliseo Vivas'.

[9] Can I say, without sounding too terribly schoolmasterish, that the usage is vulgar, simply because the man whose stock in trade is "theory" of some sort is not a "theoretician" but a "theorist"?

[10] Tate, *op. cit.,* p. 252.

[11] William J. Rooney, *The Problem of "Poetry and Belief" in Contemporary Criticism* (Washington, D.C.: Catholic University of America Press, 1949), p. 72.

[12] Archibald MacLeish, "The Language of Poetry," in *The Unity of Knowledge,* ed. Lewis Leary (Columbia University Bicentennial Conference Series [Garden City, N.Y.: Doubleday and Co., 1955]), p. 230.

[13] *Ibid.*

[14] W. H. Auden, "New Year Letter," *The Collected Poetry* (New York: Random House, 1945), p. 267.

[15] D. G. James, *Scepticism and Poetry: An Essay on the Poetic Imagination* (London: George Allen and Unwin, 1937), p. 124.

[16] Amos N. Wilder, *The Spiritual Aspects of the New Poetry* (New York: Harper & Brothers, 1940), p. 3.

[17] Stanley R. Hopper, "The Problem of Moral Isolation in Contemporary Literature," in *Spiritual Problems in Contemporary Literature,* ed. Stanley R. Hopper (New York: Harper & Brothers, 1952), p. 162.

[18] Stanley R. Hopper, *The Crisis of Faith* (Nashville: Abingdon-Cokesbury Press, 1944), p. 126.

[19] Allen Tate, *The Forlorn Demon: Didactic and Critical Essays* (Chicago: Henry Regnery Co., 1953), p. 8.

[20] Allen Tate, "Orthodoxy and the Standard of Literature," *The New Republic,* January 5, 1953, p. 24.

[21] *Vide* R. W. B. Lewis, "The Hero in the New World," *The Kenyon Review,* Vol. XIII, No. 4 (Autumn, 1951), pp. 641–660.

[22] T. S. Eliot, "Baudelaire," *Selected Essays: 1917–1932* (New York: Harcourt, Brace and Co., 1932), p. 344.

[23] Robert Penn Warren, *Brother to Dragons* (London: Eyre and Spottiswoode, 1953), p. 194.

Selected Bibliography

The check list that appears below has been arranged for the sake of readers who may want to venture further into those areas of recent criticism in which an effort is made to relate theological perspectives to issues in theory of literature and to the practical issues of discrimination in the realm of the verbal arts. The first section is devoted to "theology of culture," and here essays are listed that contribute to a definition of the cultural context in which the contemporary Christian reader encounters modern literature; the second section is devoted to works that suggest a Christian perspective upon various phases of the literary tradition; the third section is devoted to Christian assessments of modern literature; and the fourth section is devoted to essays that bear upon issues in literary theory. The check list (unlike its compiler) is itself unbiased theologically, admitting Protestant, Anglican, Roman Catholic, and Orthodox writers. But no gesture is made in the direction of comprehensiveness, for an attempt has been made to draw together only some of the materials that today seem most focal in this field and that are likely to prove most stimulating and provocative for those who have not previously made their acquaintance.

I

Berdyaev, Nicolas, *The End of Our Time*. London: Sheed and Ward, 1933.
Berdyaev, Nicolas, *The Bourgeois Mind*. New York: Sheed and Ward, 1934.
Berdyaev, Nicolas, *The Fate of Man in the Modern World*. London: S.C.M. Press, 1935.
Berdyaev, Nicolas, *The Meaning of History*. New York: Charles Scribner's Sons, 1936.
Cailliet, Émile, *The Christian Approach to Culture*. Nashville: Abingdon-Cokesbury Press, 1953.
Demant, V. A., *The Religious Prospect*. London: Frederick Muller Ltd., 1939.
Eliot, T. S., *Notes Towards the Definition of Culture*. New York: Harcourt, Brace and Co., 1949.
Hopper, Stanley R., *The Crisis of Faith*. Nashville: Abingdon-Cokesbury Press, 1944.
Maritain, Jacques, *True Humanism*. London: Geoffrey Bles, 1938.
Meland, Bernard E., *Faith and Culture*. New York: Oxford University Press, 1953.
Miller, Libuse Lukas, *The Christian and the World of Unbelief*. Nashville: Abingdon Press, 1957.

Niebuhr, Reinhold, *The Nature and Destiny of Man.* New York: Charles Scrib-
ner's Sons, 1943, 2 vols.
Roberts, Michael, *The Modern Mind.* London: Faber and Faber Ltd., 1937.
Tillich, Paul, *The Religious Situation.* New York: Henry Holt and Co., 1932.
Tillich, Paul, "The World Situation," in *The Christian Answer,* ed. H. P. Van
Dusen. New York: Charles Scribner's Sons, 1945.
Tillich, Paul, *The Protestant Era.* Chicago: University of Chicago Press, 1948.

II

Fairchild, Hoxie Neale, *Religious Trends in English Poetry.* New York: Colum-
bia University Press, Vol. I, 1939; Vol. II, 1942; Vol. III, 1949; Vol. IV, 1957.
Jarrett-Kerr, Martin, *Studies in Literature and Belief.* New York: Harper &
Brothers, 1955.
Lewis, C. S., *The Allegory of Love: A Study in Medieval Tradition.* London:
Oxford University Press, 1938.
Ross, Malcolm M., *Poetry and Dogma: The Transfiguration of Eucharistic Sym-
bols in Seventeenth Century English Poetry.* New Brunswick, N.J.: Rutgers
University Press, 1955.
Rougemont, Denis de, *Love in the Western World.* New York: Pantheon Books,
1956.
Willey, Basil, *The Seventeenth Century Background.* London: Chatto and
Windus, 1934.
Willey, Basil, *The Eighteenth Century Background.* London: Chatto and Windus,
1940.
Willey, Basil, *Nineteenth Century Studies.* London: Chatto and Windus, 1949.

III

A

(Books)

Auden, W. H., *The Enchafèd Flood, or The Romantic Iconography of the Sea.*
New York: Random House, 1950.
Bennett, Joseph D., *Baudelaire: A Criticism.* Princeton: Princeton University
Press, 1946.
Berdyaev, Nicolas, *Dostoievsky: An Interpretation.* New York: Sheed and Ward,
1934.
Bethell, S. L., *The Literary Outlook.* London: The Sheldon Press, 1943.
Eliot, T. S., *After Strange Gods: A Primer of Modern Heresy.* New York: Har-
court, Brace and Co., 1934.
Eliot, T. S., *Essays Ancient and Modern.* New York: Harcourt, Brace and Co.,
1936.
Every, Brother George, *Poetry and Personal Responsibility.* London: S.C.M.
Press Ltd., 1949.
Fowlie, Wallace, *Clowns and Angels: Studies in Modern French Literature.* New
York: Sheed and Ward, 1943.
Fowlie, Wallace, *Rimbaud.* New York: New Directions, 1946.
Fowlie, Wallace, *Jacob's Night: The Religious Renascence in France.* New York:
Sheed and Ward, 1947.

Fowlie, Wallace, *The Clown's Grail: A Study of Love in Its Literary Expression.* London: Dennis Dobson Ltd., 1947.

Gardiner, Harold C., ed., *Fifty Years of the American Novel, 1900–1950: A Christian Appraisal.* New York: Charles Scribner's Sons, 1951.

Greene, Graham, *The Lost Childhood.* New York: The Viking Press, 1952.

Jarrett-Kerr, Martin, *D. H. Lawrence and Human Existence.* London: Rockliff, 1951. (Published pseudonymously under the name Fr. William Tiverton.)

Jarrett-Kerr, Martin, *Mauriac.* New Haven: Yale University Press, 1954.

Nicholson, Norman, *Man and Literature.* London: S.C.M. Press, 1943.

Savage, D. S., *The Withered Branch: Six Studies in the Modern Novel.* New York: Pellegrini and Cudahy, n.d.

Scott, Nathan A., Jr., *Rehearsals of Discomposure: Alienation and Reconciliation in Modern Literature.* New York: King's Crown Press of Columbia University Press, 1952.

Scott, Nathan A., Jr., ed., *The Tragic Vision and the Christian Faith.* New York: Association Press, 1957.

Waggoner, Hyatt, *The Heel of Elohim: Science and Values in Modern American Poetry.* Norman, Okla.: University of Oklahoma Press, 1950.

Weidlé, Wladimir, *The Dilemma of the Arts.* London: S.C.M. Press, 1948.

Wilder, Amos N., *The Spiritual Aspects of the New Poetry.* New York: Harper & Brothers, 1940.

Wilder, Amos N., *Modern Poetry and the Christian Tradition.* New York: Charles Scribner's Sons, 1952.

B
(Essays)

Battenhouse, Roy W., "Eliot's 'The Family Reunion' as Christian Prophecy," *Christendom,* Vol. X, No. 3 (Summer, 1945).

Battenhouse, Roy W., "Shakespeare and the Tragedy of Our Time," *Theology Today,* Vol. VIII, No. 4 (January, 1952).

Battenhouse, Roy W., "Shakespearean Tragedy: A Christian Interpretation," in *The Tragic Vision and the Christian Faith,* ed. Nathan A. Scott, Jr. (New York: Association Press, 1957).

Hopper, Stanley R., "The Problem of Moral Isolation in Contemporary Literature," in *Spiritual Problems in Contemporary Literature,* ed. Stanley R. Hopper (New York: Harper & Brothers, 1952).

Hopper, Stanley R., "On the Naming of the Gods in Hölderlin and Rilke," in *Christianity and the Existentialists,* ed. Carl Michalson (New York: Charles Scribner's Sons, 1956).

Lewis, R. W. B., "The Hero in the New World: William Faulkner's *The Bear,*" *The Kenyon Review,* Vol. XIII, No. 4 (Autumn, 1951).

Marcel, Gabriel, "Rilke: A Witness to the Spiritual," *Homo Viator: Introduction to a Metaphysic of Hope* (Chicago: Henry Regnery Co., 1951).

Miller, J. Hillis, "The Creation of the Self in Gerard Manley Hopkins," *ELH, A Journal of English Literary History,* Vol. 22, No. 4 (December, 1955).

Miller, J. Hillis, "Franz Kafka and the Metaphysics of Alienation," in *The Tragic Vision and the Christian Faith,* ed. Nathan A. Scott, Jr. (New York: Association Press, 1957).

Roberts, Preston T., Jr., "Bringing Pathos into Focus," *Motive,* December, 1953.

Ross, Malcolm, "The Writer as Christian," published together with "History and Christianity: II. The Answer," by Brooks Otis, as No. 4 in the series of "Faculty Papers" published by the National Council of the Episcopal Church (281 Fourth Avenue, New York 10, N.Y.).

Scott, Nathan A., Jr., "T. S. Eliot's *The Cocktail Party:* Of Redemption and Vocation," *Religion in Life,* Vol. XX, No. 2 (Spring, 1951).

Scott, Nathan A., Jr., "Graham Greene: Christian Tragedian," *The Volusia Review,* Vol. I, No. 1 (Spring, 1954).

Scott, Nathan A., Jr., "Graham Greene: Dilemmas of the Catholic Novelist," *The Christian Century,* Vol. LXXIII, No. 31 (August 1, 1956).

Scott, Nathan A., Jr., "Dostoievsky—Tragedian of the Modern Excursion into Unbelief," in *The Tragic Vision and the Christian Faith,* ed. Nathan A. Scott, Jr. (New York: Association Press, 1957).

Scott, Nathan A., Jr., "Edna St. Vincent Millay: A Reconsideration," *The Christian Century,* Vol. LXXIV, No. 18 (May 1, 1957).

Stewart, Randall, "American Literature and the Christian Tradition," published as a "Faculty Paper" by the National Council of the Episcopal Church in 1955.

Stewart, Randall, "The Vision of Evil in Hawthorne and Melville," in *The Tragic Vision and the Christian Faith,* ed. Nathan A. Scott, Jr. (New York: Association Press, 1957).

Traversi, D. A., "Dostoievsky," *The Criterion,* Vol. XVI, No. LXV (July, 1937).

Waggoner, Hyatt H., "William Faulkner's Passion Week of the Heart," in *The Tragic Vision and the Christian Faith,* ed. Nathan A. Scott, Jr. (New York: Association Press, 1957).

IV

A

(Books)

Bethell, S. L., *Literary Criticism.* London: Dennis Dobson Ltd., 1948.

Bremond, Henri, *Prayer and Poetry.* London: Burns, Oates and Washbourne Ltd., 1927.

Every, Brother George, *Christian Discrimination.* London: The Sheldon Press, 1940.

Gilby, Thomas, *Poetic Experience.* New York: Sheed and Ward, 1934.

Henn, T. R., *The Harvest of Tragedy.* London: Methuen and Co., Ltd., 1956.

La Tour du Pin, Patrice de, *The Dedicated Life in Poetry.* London: The Harvill Press, 1948.

MacGregor, Geddes, *Aesthetic Experience in Religion.* London: Macmillan & Co., Ltd., 1947.

Maritain, Jacques, *Art and Poetry.* New York: Philosophical Library, 1943.

Maritain, Jacques, *Art and Scholasticism.* New York: Charles Scribner's Sons, 1943.

Maritain, Jacques, *Creative Intuition in Art and Poetry.* New York: Pantheon Books, 1953.

Maritain, Jacques, and Cocteau, Jean, *Art and Faith.* New York: Philosophical Library, 1948.

Maritain, Jacques, and Maritain, Raissa, *The Situation of Poetry*. New York: Philosophical Library, 1955.

McCarron, Hugh, *Realization: A Philosophy of Poetry*. London: Sheed and Ward, 1937.

Murray, Rosalind, *The Forsaken Fountain*. New York: Longmans, Green and Co., 1948.

Pointing, Horace B., *Art, Religion and the Common Life*. London: S.C.M. Press Ltd., 1947.

Pottle, Frederick A., *The Idiom of Poetry*. Ithaca, N.Y.: Cornell University Press, 1946.

Rooney, William J., *The Problem of "Poetry and Belief" in Contemporary Criticism*. Washington, D.C.: Catholic University of America Press, 1949.

Tate, Allen, *The Forlorn Demon: Didactic and Critical Essays*. Chicago: Henry Regnery Co., 1953.

Thomas, George F., *Poetry, Religion, and the Spiritual Life*. Houston: Elsevier Press, 1951.

Turnell, Martin, *Poetry and Crisis*. London: Sands, The Paladin Press, 1938.

B
(Essays)

Auden, W. H., "The Christian Tragic Hero," *The New York Times Book Review*, December 16, 1945.

Auden, W. H., "Squares and Oblongs," in *Poets at Work*, ed. C. D. Abbot (New York: Harcourt, Brace and Co., 1948).

Auden, W. H., "The Ironic Hero," *Horizon*, Vol. XX, No. 116 (August, 1949).

Auden, W. H., "Nature, History and Poetry," *Thought*, Vol. XXV (1951), pp. 412-422.

Auden, W. H., "Notes on the Comic," *Thought*, Vol. XXVII (1952), pp. 57-71.

Auden, W. H., "Balaam and the Ass: The Master-Servant Relation in Literature," *Thought*, Vol. XXXIX (1954), pp. 237-270.

Auden, W. H., *Making, Knowing and Judging*. Oxford: Clarendon Press, 1956.

Battenhouse, Roy W., "The Relation of Theology to Literary Criticism," *The Journal of Bible and Religion*, Vol. XIII, No. 1 (February, 1945).

Brooks, Cleanth, "Metaphor and the Function of Criticism," in *Spiritual Problems in Contemporary Literature*, ed. Stanley R. Hopper (New York: Harper & Brothers, 1952).

Cameron, J. M., "Poetry and Metaphysics," *The Dublin Review*, No. 220 (Autumn, 1947).

Coleburt, R., "The Poet and the Philosopher," *The Downside Review*, Vol. 68 (January, 1950).

Donahue, Charles, "Literary Criticism and Philosophy," *Thought*, Vol. 26, No. 103 (Winter, 1951–52).

Fairchild, Hoxie Neale, *Religious Perspectives of College Teaching in English Literature*. New Haven, Conn.: The Edward W. Hazen Foundation, 1950 (a Hazen Pamphlet). Reprinted in *Religious Perspectives of College Teaching*, ed. Hoxie Neale Fairchild (New York: Ronald Press, 1952).

Jenkinson, R. S., "Towards a Christian Aesthetic," *The Downside Review*, Vol. 67, No. 207 (Winter, 1948–49).

Knight, Douglas, "Religious Implications in the Humanities," in *Liberal Learning and Religion,* ed. Amos N. Wilder (New York: Harper & Brothers, 1951).

Lewis, H. D., "Revelation and Art," *Proceedings of the Aristotelian Society,* Supplemental Volume XXIII. Reprinted in H. D. Lewis, *Morals and Revelation* (London: George Allen and Unwin, Ltd., 1951).

Lynch, William F., "Theology and the Imagination," *Thought,* Vol. XXIX, No. 112 (Spring, 1954); Vol. XXIX, No. 115 (Winter, 1954–55); and Vol. XXX, No. 116 (Spring, 1955).

Ong, Walter J., "Art and Mystery: A Revaluation," *Speculum,* Vol. XXII (July, 1947).

Roberts, David E., "Christian Faith and Greek Tragedy," *Religion in Life,* Vol. XVIII, No. 1 (Winter, 1948–49).

Roberts, Preston T., "A Christian Theory of Dramatic Tragedy," *The Journal of Religion,* Vol. XXXI, No. 1 (January, 1951).

Rougemont, Denis de, "Religion and the Mission of the Artist," in *Spiritual Problems in Contemporary Literature,* ed. Stanley R. Hopper (New York: Harper & Brothers, 1952).

Sayers, Dorothy L., "Towards a Christian Aesthetic," *Unpopular Opinions: Twenty-One Essays* (New York: Harcourt, Brace and Co., 1947).

Scott, Nathan A., Jr., "A Neglected Aspect of the Theological Curriculum," *The Journal of Religious Thought,* Vol. VII, No. 1 (Autumn-Winter, 1949–50).

Scott, Nathan A., Jr., "Lionel Trilling's Critique of the Liberal Mind," *Christianity and Society,* Vol. XVI, No. 2 (Spring, 1951).

Scott, Nathan A., Jr., "The Relation of Theology to Literary Criticism," *The Journal of Religion,* Vol. XXXIII, No. 4 (October, 1953).

Scott, Nathan A., Jr., "Poetry and the Crisis of Metaphysics," *The Christian Scholar,* Vol. XXXVI, No. 4 (December, 1953).

Scott, Nathan A., Jr., "Religious Implications in the Humanities," *The Journal of Human Relations,* Vol. II, No. 2 (Winter, 1954).

Scott, Nathan A., Jr., "The Realism of Erich Auerbach," *The Christian Scholar,* Vol. XXXVII, No. 4 (December, 1954).

Scott, Nathan A., Jr., "Maritain in His Role as Aesthetician," *The Review of Metaphysics,* Vol. VIII, No. 3 (March, 1955).

Sewell, Elizabeth, "The Death of the Imagination," *Thought,* Vol. XXVIII (Autumn, 1953).

Wimsatt, W. K., "Poetry and Christian Thinking," *The Verbal Icon* (Lexington: University of Kentucky Press, 1954).

Index

Set in Linotype Granjon
Format by Norma Stahl
Manufactured by The Haddon Craftsmen, Inc.
Published by HARPER & BROTHERS, *New York*